AMERICAN DESIGNERS' HOUSES

JUDITH KRANTZ
Jet Set
GORKY PARK
SLAVES of NEW YORK
Garson Kanin | Tracy and Hepburn
FINANCIALLY SUCCESSFUL YOUR OWN BUSINESS
SOMEONE ELSE'S MONEY
INDECENT EXPOSURE
BOND RISK ANALYSIS

AMERICAN DESIGNERS' HOUSES

DOMINIC BRADBURY
Photography
MARK LUSCOMBE-WHYTE

The Vendome Press

TO MY MOTHER

First published in the United States of America by
The Vendome Press
1334 York Avenue
New York, NY 10021

ISBN: 0–86565–227–9

Library of Congress Cataloging-in-Publication Data

Bradbury, Dominic.
American designers' houses / Dominic Bradbury; photographs by Mark Luscombe-Whyte.
p. cm.
Includes bibliographical references and index.
ISBN 0-86565-227-9 (hardcover: alk. paper)
1. Interior decorators–Homes and haunts–United States. 2. Interior decoration–United States. I. Luscombe-Whyte, Mark. II. Title.
NK2115.3.I57B73 2004
747'.0973–dc22
2004049603

Front cover image: Mica Ertegün; back cover images: left: Mica Ertegün; centre: Juan Pablo Molyneux; right: Thomas Pheasant; half-title page: Mica Ertegün; title page: Muriel Brandolini; contents page: Holly Hunt.

Reproduction by: Classicscan Pte Ltd, Singapore
Printed by: SNP Leefung, China

contents

Introduction

The draw of the USA is as strong as ever. That's especially true of American design and architecture, with its striking openness, energy, and breadth. There is a sense in which American design has always looked outwards, across the world, to bring together a disparate set of inspirations and influences within a body of work that is powerfully fresh and original, vibrant and alive, and definitively American. There is an awareness of history, of the past, and of tradition, yet designers in the States have looked more than most to make it new, forging ahead through innovation and experimentation.

The country has long had a deep allure for all those with creative and original minds. That was especially true of the 1930s and 1940s when upheaval in Europe saw many of its architectural and design pioneers emigrating to the States. Among them were leaders and disciples of the Bauhaus and the modern movement, such as Mies van der Rohe, Walter Gropius, Josef Albers, László Moholy-Nagy. Louis Kahn was born in Estonia, Richard Neutra was Austrian by birth, Eero Saarinen was Finnish, I.M Pei was born in China. They helped to place the USA at the forefront of modernist architecture, joining the ranks of a homegrown elite including Frank Lloyd Wright, Charles Eames, and John Lautner. There was a powerful fusion of ideas expressed on a landscape and cityscape that was perhaps less encumbered by tradition than was the case in Europe, more open to experiment and new expressions of form and line.

Many of these designers and architects were multi-talented, working with architecture, interiors, furniture, and other products. Their frame of reference was vast, their bank of experience varied and rich. The USA offered support and space, resources, and a freedom from many of the pressures and restrictions – some of them economic, some political, some artistic – that they had experienced in other countries. Collectively, the pioneers of modernism pushed through a revolution in design centred upon the States which became a source of inspiration to all who followed.

OPPOSITE The main living room of interior designer Lee Mindel's penthouse apartment, overlooking the New York skyline. The black armchairs are by Jules Leleu, the tall chair by Poul Henningsen, with rugs by V'Soske.

ABOVE Bold horizontal stripes enliven the walls of Muriel Brandolini's house in the Hamptons; Brandolini is best known for her use of colour and pattern. The long multi-tone sofa is by Pierre Charpin, with tables from Albrizzi, and bookcases by Andrea Branzi.

Within the sphere of contemporary interior design, there has been another great enrichment of the discipline by a similar combination of incomers, insiders, and iconoclasts who have placed American interiors at the forefront of the design world. One thinks of Juan Montoya and Juan Pablo Molyneux from South America, Benjamin Noriega-Ortiz and Vicente Wolf from the Caribbean, Kathryn Ireland, Mica Ertegun, and Muriel Brandolini from parts of Europe, Calvin Tsao from Asia and Karim Rashid, born in North Africa and who arrived in the States via Canada and Britain. The depth and breadth of these designers' imaginations and resourcefulness has added many new dimensions to the collective strength and vigour of American design.

This influx of ideas and talent from around the world has led to a strong fusion strand within American design, a blending of a complex, diverse collection box of themes and variations, from Asia, Europe, South America, Africa, and beyond. These are designers with an international perspective and work load, often with second homes abroad and a frenetic travel schedule, who layer their work with fabrics, materials, furniture, and salvage sourced in a global market place. Yet there is still a sensibility and an awareness within their work which is essentially American and builds on a powerful 20th-century foundation in American design, with an emphasis on originality, a lack of pretension or snobbishness, and liberty and licence in expression.

Before the 20th century, the USA seemed all too ready to look back to Europe, especially England and France, for a lead in interior design and architecture. The iconic decorator Elsie de Wolfe was one of the first in the States to begin to clear away the clutter and overbearing heaviness of Victorian home style and forge the way for a cleaner, fresher approach, albeit still rooted in tradition. Later, designers such as Frances Elkins and Dorothy Draper took another step forward, establishing interior design on a more

ABOVE A calm composition in one corner of New York designer Vicente Wolf's loft apartment. His love of collecting photography is in evidence as well as his own furniture designs, with sofa and club chair by Wolf set around a Giacometti inspired table.

professional footing and experimenting with colour and form. Billy Baldwin, who died in 1983, was perhaps the most influential American decorator of the 20th century, combining classical and modernist influences with an open and erudite attitude to colour, eclecticism and comfort. Like David Hicks in England, he took tradition and modernity and drew them together with passion, learning, and sensitivity to create something altogether new and contemporary.

Other designers, such as Rose Cumming and Tony Duquette, trod a path that was far more theatrical and flamboyant. The careers of a number of the heirs to Baldwin and Hicks, for example Angelo Donghia, Mark Hampton, and Jed Johnson, were sadly cut short in the 1990s, robbing American design of key voices. Yet there was still the great example of Parish–Hadley, where the traditionalism of Sister Parish was balanced and enhanced by the learned modernity of Albert Hadley (see pages 68–75), and a whole new swathe of young designers with talent, originality and ambitions, looking outwards and forwards.

The twenty designers in this book represent a broad spectrum of contemporary American interior design and a range of sensibilities and aesthetic approaches, from the neo-traditionalism of David Easton or Joanne de Guardiola through to the exuberant fresh modernity of Karim Rashid or the pared-down prowess of Lee Mindel or Tsao & McKown. Yet, with the international outlook and broad backgrounds of these American designers, there is perhaps a sense in which all are exponents of fusion design and architecture.

Similar to those pioneering modernists, these are also interior designers whose talents stretch across many disciplines and fields. Many are also architects, or have a strong architectural background, from Lee Mindel to Tsao McKown to Juan Montoya, Benjamin Noriega-Ortiz and David Easton. Like Thomas Pheasant, Rose Tarlow, Kathryn Ireland, and Sills Huniford, they are furniture and fabric designers, with their own collections, parallel businesses, and a way of mixing creativity with energy and business acumen. Others are painters and artists.

BELOW The boundaries between inside and out are blurred within the twin porches at David Easton's country house, an hour's drive from New York. Here a chaise longue by Easton sits alongside a plant stand that graced Billy Baldwin's Nantucket home.

"A lot of the early modernists were somewhat renaissance and broad," says Karim Rashid, "but by post World War II we were moving into an age of specialization and the demise of the Buckminster Fullers of the world. But it's in most creative people to cross the boundaries and try your hand at many different things. I think we are going to see more and more of this blurring again."

Indeed, the new breed of American designers have taken interior design to a new level. They understand that design is both business and art, commerce and craft. They are aware of the power of marketing and image, of advertising and publicity. They have an awareness of fashion and shifting trends, but refuse to be dictated by them. They understand tradition and draw upon it, yet seek to break down conventions and reinterpret our built environment. They are always asking questions and looking for new answers.

ABOVE Light bathes the dining room of Thomas Pheasant's Parisian escape. Most of the furniture in the renovated period apartment was designed by Pheasant himself, including the screen and day bed. The painting is by Richard Serra.

Here, the creativity and convention-defying nature of the work of many of America's leading designers is expressed upon the canvas of their own homes. These are individual laboratories of design, arenas where a designer's taste and style can have free reign and pure execution, reflecting personality and artistic accomplishment. They represent a spirit of invention and innovation that is beyond fashion, more enduring and distinctive.

"I'm proud to be considered an American designer," says Stephen Sills, of Sills Huniford, "because I think they are the best decorators in the world. They are more original and they have less to work with, because there is very little great architecture in this country. They have to be more inventive with what they have to work with. They are the best."

classic

Juan Pablo Molyneux

LIVING ABOVE THE SHOP HAS BECOME SOMETHING OF A TRADITION FOR JUAN PABLO MOLYNEUX. IT BEGAN AT HIS HOME IN BUENOS AIRES. IN NEW YORK HE COMBINES HOME AND OFFICE WITHIN A BEAUX ARTS TOWNHOUSE OFF MADISON AVENUE. AND THE SAME IS NOW TRUE OF HIS HOUSE IN PARIS, AN EARLY 17TH-CENTURY BUILDING IN THE THIRD ARRONDISEMENT. THE EUROPEAN OFFICE AND STUDIO OF MOLYNEUX'S DESIGN AND ARCHITECTURAL PRACTICE INHABITS PART OF THIS SYMPATHETICALLY RESTORED BUILDING, WHILE THE DESIGNER AND HIS WIFE, PILAR, MAKE THEIR HOME ALONGSIDE.

"Throughout my entire life it's been the same thing," says Molyneux, "perhaps because in my mind it's impossible to dissociate work and rest, and rest and work. If I'm working on a project I love to come into my office on a Sunday morning, in my bathrobe or jeans, and go through the drawings. I can go to work just by taking the elevator or the staircase."

The Molyneuxs bought the building in 2001, or the majority of it. It was a rare opportunity to buy such a large and cohesive home in the heart of Paris, although it had been much altered and subdivided over the centuries. Juan Pablo Molyneux had been renting an apartment in the city for some years, but found that his work brought him to Europe so regularly that a more permanent arrangement would be better. "It's a link that's been hard to keep but I fight for it," he says. "I never wanted to feel that I didn't belong here, even if I just had a little *pied-à-terre* somewhere."

OPPOSITE The upstairs library contains a hidden door among the bookshelves leading through to the master bedroom and other adjoining rooms. The walls are covered in chenille while the round table is 18th-century English.

The building dates back to 1619 and was occupied during the French Revolution. Some parts of the structure were demolished and lost, including the grand staircase, as it had been divided up into a series of apartments. Molyneux's first intention was to clean up the house and recreate a flavour of what the building

OPPOSITE The salon leads to the new stairway, designed by Molyneux, to create a sense of grandeur and an appropriate sense of scale within a limited space. The statue is a marble copy of the bronze Egyptian figure of Anthonious from Pavlosk.

was like before the Revolution. One part of the house had original painted ceilings and beams, and was restored. For the rest, only the bare bones remained.

"For me it was very important that I take care of this ailing piece of history and make it proud again," Molyneux says. "My major challenge was to create a main staircase to the first floor because the only spaces I had to work with were quite narrow and the ceilings extremely high, which would create a very awkward staircase. So the design of the staircase took almost the entire width of the hallway for the first step, then I 'strangled' the staircase in the curve and went back to the full width upstairs. It tricks the eye and creates a very grand staircase in a very narrow room. The other important thing is that I used a traditional manner of construction called *escalier de saracène*, which is self-supporting with one stone supporting another."

As Molyneux was piecing the building back together and working on the plans of the house, he realized that there was a basement space that was

ABOVE A detail of the ground floor salon with a photograph by Doug Hall, from a series depicting opera houses, in this case the Teatro de la Fortuna. The marble console and vases tie in with the chequer board marble floor and the painted walls.

LEFT The ground floor salon is united by a cool, classical palette of materials and references. The mirror is 18th-century Venetian with Roman marble medallions above the doorways. The silk velvet upholstery of the sofa softens the stonework.

unaccounted for and without any access. Investigation showed that there was a series of original arched cellars, which had been closed at some point during the building's lifetime. It was a convenient discovery, which meant that services could be hidden down in the basement, while there was also enough room for a small wine cellar and a more informal reception room.

The studio takes up a large part of the ground floor, with an adjoining formal reception salon designed in a relatively restrained version of Molyneux's distinctive "modern neo-classicism," with a chequerboard stone floor, largely neutral colour palette, and classical flourishes. Upstairs, within the more private part of the home, the designer's taste for opulence and exuberance, as well as touches of humour, fantasy, and theatricality, becomes more apparent.

The dining room is a conversation piece in itself, with the walls painted in elegant *singerie* depicting the story of Molyneux's own life together with that

BELOW The theatrical painted singerie panels in the dining room tell the story of the Molyneuxs' meeting and shared life together. The dining chairs are 19th- century Italian.

RIGHT A view of the Chinese lacquered hall, looking back through the main salon to the library, with the marble centurion standing on its plinth. The "hallway" also serves as a flexible room, open to a choice of furniture.

of his wife. The room echoes the dining room of his Manhattan townhouse, detailed in *singerie* of a more abstract nature.

"It has a naive charm but also humour," says Molyneux. "I have lunch there by myself sometimes and I am so amused because wherever you put your eye you have to smile. You can go with the strictest form of architecture but I don't believe it can achieve something successful in the contemporary manner without humour. Anything that has humour creates an easy rapport between building and person."

The grand salon is dominated by 17th- and 18th-century tapestries, hanging on crimson, fabric-coated walls. Together with the rugs over the parquet, the window seats, and flowing curtains, this is a soft, warm evening room, bathed in colour. Next door is the Chinese hallway, a flexible space also rich with deep red tones.

BELOW The main living room, upstairs, is the focal point of the Molyneuxs' home. The walls are coated in a seductive chenille, upon which have been mounted a series of 17th-century tapestries. The tables are by Diego Giacometti.

ABOVE LEFT The winding staircase starts with a wide step, narrows and opens out again to reconnect the two floors of the house in a confined space. The stair rail itself is 18th century, while to one side stands a marble column and taza.

ABOVE RIGHT The guest bedroom stands at the opposite end of the house to the master bedroom, creating a sense of privacy. The walls are covered in a yellow silk damask, with an engraving by Charles Le Brun. The bed is in a Chippendale style and is upholstered in silk velvet.

"My life is full of colour. If I can say I will be known for something, then it's colour, and I'm certainly not afraid of it," Molyneux believes. "And in most of my interiors I try to leave the possibility of flexibility. With the chinoiserie room, I love the idea of putting a round table in there and having dinner, or just having a chair and listening to music or reading. Or to leave it just as a hall. It is the most tranquil room you can be in."

The sensitivity of the overall restoration is not only in tune with the building itself but the Parisian context. It is a city which has long fascinated Molyneux, who studied at the Ecole des Beaux-Arts in the 1960s, following on

ABOVE The master bedroom sits next to the library, with windows overlooking the internal courtyard of the building. The bed is bespoke, while the armchairs and side table are 19th-century Russian, with a 17th-century screen.

from a degree in architecture at Santiago's Catholic University in his native Chile. The neo-classical grandeur of Paris made a deep impression, surpassing his interest in modernism and reinforcing his belief in the key architectural principles of harmony, proportion, symmetry, and rhythm.

"Those years were a very important and predominant influence. And they were so influential because I wanted to participate and be part of it all, as I am now, rather than just an observer. And when I was studying in Paris, when I was nineteen, I drove my Deux Chevaux to Saint Petersburg, which was quite a trip. Ever since, I have also had a love affair with that city. Paris and Saint

ABOVE In the guest bathroom, the trellis mirror-work in a bronze frame helps reflect light and create the illusion of a space with far larger proportions. Yet the limited palette of colours and materials also creates the impression of simplicity.

Petersburg are really a master lesson in classicism. You can't go to any other school that could teach you the magnificence of neo-classicism so effectively."

Having finished his studies, Molyneux returned to Chile and began working as an interior and furniture designer. But he had always had an ambivalent relationship with Chile, unenamoured of its colonial architecture and constantly looking beyond its borders, even as a child when he went to an English school with occasional semesters in Britain. So from the start there was this peripatetic spirit. At 26 Molyneux staged an exhibition of his work at the National Museum in Santiago and then left for Argentina.

"I did some important commercial work in Argentina, as well as residential," he says, "and perhaps that was the place of my true formation as a designer because it was all about my knowledge applied to reality. And fortunately it was in a land like Argentina, which has a certain level of *savoir-faire*. But even then I travelled a lot and always kept in contact with my sources in Europe and New York. So moving to America was a natural step and when we arrived in New York I instantly had the feeling of being at home. It was one of those magical things; everything started right."

Through a mixture of word and mouth, as well as the support of influential magazines such as *Architectural Digest*, Molyneux rapidly established himself in North America. New York was home, but his work held him to the life of the constant traveller, taking him to Canada, Europe, and back to Saint Petersburg. He cultivates what he sees as a vital relationship between architecture and interiors, as well as landscape design, within highly cohesive and individual projects, grounded in neoclassicism but with a love of playfulness and surprises, tricking the eye with scale and proportion. And he has an acute awareness, not only of modernism but of the contemporary demands of today's lifestyles.

ABOVE The discovery of a hidden basement created the opportunity to not only create a small wine cellar and hide away essential services, but also to create an alternative salon, with a striking ensemble of horn-and-fur sofa and chairs.

"One thing I never forget is that we are living in the 21st century," Molyneux says. "My style used to be very modern and then, the more I thought of the weight of neoclassical heritage, culture, and knowledge, that changed. It went through the strainer of modernism and I added certain elements and it became a vision of modern neo-classicism. It's putting interiors together with a contemporary eye without forgetting the human need for comfort, warmth, art. For instance, in my Paris home I was able to create a contemporary room like the salon with the check marble floor and antique pieces but combined with Giacometti furniture and a Doug Hall photograph. Evidently we can do something much more modern than that, but it's introducing the appropriate degree of fresh air into an 17th-century building."

David Easton

THERE IS A SMALL CARD PINNED UP BY DAVID EASTON'S DESK IN THE STUDY OF HIS COUNTRY HOME, OUT IN ROCKLAND COUNTY, AN HOUR'S DRIVE FROM NEW YORK CITY. "FORTUNATE TOO IS THAT MAN WHO HAS COME TO KNOW THE GODS OF THE COUNTRYSIDE," READS THE CARD, CREDITING VIRGIL. IT SEEMS PARTICULARLY APPOSITE HERE, WITH THE HOUSE THAT EASTON AND HIS PARTNER, ARTIST JAMES STEINMEYER, HAVE BUILT FOR THEMSELVES, SURROUNDED BY UNDULATING WOODLANDS AND CROWNED BY A QUIET COURTYARD GARDEN. THIS IS A TRUE ESCAPE FROM THE CITY AND ITS PRESSURES.

"We first came up here one Memorial Day around 1985 and we walked around and were fascinated by the mood of the place," says Easton. "We were staying with some friends nearby and they had heard the land and gardens were for sale. It was a ramshackle place and the gardens had become very overgrown but there was a definite spirit to it. We bought it almost immediately."

What Easton was buying was the remains of a garden – including an old garden house – laid out around 1918 by an influential horticulturalist and garden writer by the name of Louise Beebe Wilder. Together with her husband, architect Walter Wilder, she created the enclosed courtyard garden and lived in a farmhouse nearby, both part of a 220-acre farm known as Balderbrae. The garden, with its pergolas and vast planted pots and ornaments, became the focus of Beebe Wilder's work and was recorded in one of her best known books, *Colour in my Garden*.

By the 1980s the garden was in a sorry state, but the bones of it still remained, and when David Easton first saw the site his imagination went to work. He pictured a country house positioned along the northern wall of the garden, opposite the old garden house, which has itself since been restored

OPPOSITE Lined with bookshelves, the master bedroom is generously proportioned enough to also serve as a library, as well as a more intimate sitting room. By the window stands a Swedish table and a pair of English armchairs.

as a two-bedroom guest lodge. The main house was realized with a vast, double height, open-plan living and dining room at its heart, with French windows opening out on to the courtyard garden. It is a series of compositions and arrangements, layered with blue-and-white delft china and an eclectic but cohesive mix of period furniture from France, England, Sweden, and Spain, all within one large, elegant and almost barn-like space, built in stone, topped by a modest clocktower and adorned with green shutters.

"We decided we didn't want a formal house, but something that looked comfortable in the country," says Easton. "And I had also become tired of the living room, the dining room, the billiard room, the this and the that. So we built this one room which, after summers in France and Italy, seemed a nice way to live, and so we have a fireplace at either end, with seating at one and dining at the other."

ABOVE The main living room is a series of compositions and arrangements, each with its own focus and heart. Here a Delft vase from Easton's collection of blue-and-white china sit on top of a table bought from dealer Christopher Gibbs in London.

OPPOSITE The living room is a multi-functional space with barn-like height and proportions. Arranged around the fireplace at the far end of the room is a seating area with a pair of Louis XV chairs covered in a Colefax & Fowler fabric.

Wings were added to each side of this dramatic focal point, one housing kitchen and utility areas and the other the study, followed by a master bedroom and bathroom to the rear, set back from the rest of the house. This bedroom, too, benefits from a high ceiling and a generosity of space, a series of inset library bookcases and its own seating area, with French-inspired boudoir chairs arranged around a large fireplace, topped by an Italianate mirror.

"It's an easy house to live in," says Easton, who also has an apartment in the Flat Iron district of New York, partly touched by an open-plan, loft-like approach mixed with classical flourishes and period pieces. "It's very comfortable house and there's always a place to sit, a place to put a drink down. And there's a sensibility about soft colour and the use of texture and all those things that go into any house that we do, no matter what its style, as well as a sensibility about the place where it is."

Projecting out from the two wings of the house into the courtyard garden is a pair of long porches that help to frame part of the garden, while also forming summer rooms in themselves. The porch by the entrance to the kitchen forms an alternative dining area, and is furnished with a pair of circular dining tables, while the other is a semi-enclosed sitting room, complete with fireplace and rattan furniture. Circular windows at the garden end of each of the two

verandahs offer choice views down through the restored pergolas, each one formed from a dozen towering columns, to the god-head fountains encased in the walls beyond.

"I really grew up with porches," says Easton. "My grandparents had two porches and at night everyone sat out there in front of the house before and after dinner. My parents had a screen porch and the rattan furniture we have came from their house. In a way, everything comes from our past."

Easton was born in Kentucky, but grew up in Pennsylvania. His father was a businessman and the family lived in a traditional brick home with a central

BELOW Between the twin doorways leading through to the kitchen and reception hall stands another fireplace, with the dining table close by. The dining table itself is Swedish, while the mirror above the French fireplace is 17th-century Spanish.

hall. He recognized his vocation from an early age, furtively drawing and designing houses at the back of the classroom, whatever the lesson. His grandparents lived just outside Chicago and Easton well remembers time spent in the city as a child, heading to Marshall Field's department store where, on the seventh floor, they had antiques and four show houses that you could walk right through. Then there were the Thorne miniature rooms at the Art Institute of Chicago. "They were so exquisitely done and as a kid you could stand by the rail and follow architecture from early English or American through to modern New York or Paris."

BELOW A series of French windows allow light to flood into the living room from the enclosed garden beyond. The two cabinets by the windows are by David Easton, as are the stools – covered in a Lee Jofa fabric – around the central circular table.

ABOVE Like the sitting room, the master bedroom has a high ceiling and a good sense of scale. A seating area, with French boudoir-style armchairs by Easton, is arranged around the fireplace. The bed is 19th-century French.

Chicago also offered a timely introduction to the work of architect David Adler, whose houses – particularly the Armor House in Lake Forest – were a great influence then and now. "He was a classical architect," notes Easton. "But his houses had that Vitruvian issue of commodity, firmness, and delight. Adler was certainly an inspiration."

Easton went on to study architecture at the Pratt Institute in Brooklyn, where Sibyl Moholy-Nagy was teaching at the time. She became another major influence, because of her passion for architecture while at the same time passing on her understanding of the broad history of architecture. After Pratt, Easton spent five years in New York working in architectural practices until he realized that his preference was for interiors. He took a formative five-month scholarship trip to Europe, extending a stay at Fontainebleau with a personal "grand tour" that also took in England, Italy, and Scandinavia.

When he returned from Europe he took up a job with furniture designer Edward Wormley and then moved to Parish-Hadley – which had become a designer's finishing school of a kind, attracting a swathe of rising stars serving their apprenticeships – where he stayed for eighteen months.

"I watched the magic of Albert Hadley and Sister Parish working together and they were certainly an influence," Easton says. "It taught me a certain awareness about comfort, the placement of furniture and its relationship to people using a room, and the sense of a room as a series of mini-environments and how you then break them up and make them look attractive."

In 1972 Easton set up on his own, rapidly establishing a reputation for interiors grounded in neo-classicism; houses that not only drew heavily on the look of the traditional English country house and Old-World style, but also included a sensitivity to more contemporary and informal ways of living, as well as to context and setting. His defining project became the cohesive restoration of an epic Virginia estate called Albemarle, begun in the 1980s for the Kluge family, including a house, chapel, stables, log cabin, and now a vineyard building and farm store, all in classical style.

Having formed a business partnership with decorator Charlotte Moss, Easton's work has taken him across North America, down to Mexico and across to Europe, with his office handling both architecture and interiors. His portfolio now also includes fabric collections for Lee Jofa and a furniture line for Henredon, as Easton continues to expand his range and repertoire.

Certainly, though remaining very much a classicist, Easton has always been open to change and new thinking. As well as Soane and Schinkel, Easton has a passion for Barragan, Frank Lloyd Wright, and Frank Gehry. His houses, including his own, recognize that ways of living move on, that priorities shift, and that increasingly we demand greater flexibility and informality.

ABOVE A detail of a wall-mounted model house in the master bedroom, bought at auction, stands above a detail of one of the bedrooms in the guest cottage – a retreat that lies opposite the main house, with the pool and enclosed garden between.

RIGHT A detail of a porthole window in one the porches, looking outwards and down through one of the garden pergolas towards the guest house and the wall fountains to either side of it. The gardens promote a sense of symmetry and order.

BELOW One of the twin porches, which project outwards from the wings of the main house and help enclose the garden. One of the porches is used as a summer "sitting room" and this one – nearest to the kitchen – as an indoor/outdoor dining area.

There is the feeling at Easton's home in Rockland County, with its stone and clapboard and lovingly restored gardens, that it must have been there for centuries, given that it sits so naturally into its surroundings, blending period pieces from around the world. But looking more closely one also sees the modernity of it, with its multi-functional spaces and lack of pretension.

"I think Falling Water is the most extraordinary house of the 20th century and Gehry's Guggenheim Bilbao the greatest building of our age," says Easton. "But even in the most modern house or apartment that we do, I'll never be able to leave classicism behind because I wouldn't feel comfortable. I will always have one foot in the past."

BELOW The swimming pool makes a welcome addition within the lower terrace of the walled garden, near to the guest house. The central section of the main house, capped by a clock tower, holds the central living room with wings and porches to either side.

Rose Tarlow

YOU COULD SAY THAT ROSE TARLOW'S HOME IS A GRAND ILLUSION. WALKING INTO HER EXTRAORDINARY BEL AIR HOUSE, NESTLING AMONG THE TREES ON A QUIET HILLSIDE, ONE IMAGINES THAT IT HAS BEEN HERE FOR CENTURIES. BOSTON IVY CREEPS IN ACROSS THE WALLS AND CEILING OF THE VAST CENTRAL SITTING ROOM, WHERE MEDIEVAL OAK BEAMS HIGH ABOVE YOU SUPPORT THE ROOF LINE. AT EITHER END OF THE ROOM ARE 17TH-CENTURY BARONIAL FRENCH FIREPLACES. YET THIS MOSAIC OF ARCHITECTURAL SALVAGE, ANTIQUES AND ARTWORK, WAS CONCEIVED AND BUILT IN JUST 14 MONTHS.

"I love thinking of it as a puzzle," says Tarlow. "I like puzzles and playing with plans. I can work on the floor plans for a room for hours, over and over, and I find it so stimulating. The paper part of designing a house is what I actually like best, much better than building. Within the conceptual aspect of creation you have total control but inevitably when you start the building process that's taken away. And it was the first house I did on my own and for myself that I really built from nothing. I don't know if anything can be better than that feeling for your first love."

In planning the house, which replaced a semi-derelict building on the narrow site, she studied the houses of Wallace Neff, a revivalist architect who worked in Los Angeles in the 1920s and 1930s. Neff designed homes for, among others, Douglas Fairbanks and Mary Pickford, with a strong sense of the picturesque and a vivid European influence, particularly French and Italian.

The layout of Tarlow's house was partly dictated by the site itself, but also by the desire to create an axis living room, which gets used all the time, with an adjoining master bedroom. The dining room and kitchen are accessed through the doorway in the opposite corner, formed from one of four pairs of 18th-century French oak doors used in the sitting room. All of this part of the house

OPPOSITE One of two 17th century French stone fireplaces incorporated at either end of the large, central living room. The drawing above the fireplace is by Jean Cocteau, drawn on a wall in Paris and then removed and framed.

ABOVE The living room is also library and gallery, cradling many collections and compositions. To the right stands a Spanish table with a Richard Serra painting balanced on top. The shelves hold a collection of Roman glass, as well as books.

is on one level, but there is a stairway off the main entrance hall that takes you to guest rooms and a studio within a two-storey section of the house.

The proportion and scale of these interrelated spaces is striking, especially the pivotal living room, lined with bookcases filled with volumes on an array of architectural and artistic subjects from Aalto to Tadao Ando and French chateaux to Russian houses. The inspiration for each room comes from antiques or salvaged gems, such as the beams in the living room or the French pine panelling in the master bedroom, which become spurs to Tarlow's imagination.

"One or two things usually inspire a room for me," she says, "and until I find those it doesn't really come together. In a sense I don't see myself as a decorator because I really need that inspiration to get things done. And my taste is very masculine, for pieces that are strong and large scale. A bedroom could be different, but the rest of the house needs to flow well and so the experience as you move from room to room shouldn't be too different. The height and scale of rooms might change, but everything else should be harmonious. I don't like to feel as though different rooms in a house are completely separate design elements."

ABOVE Vines creep in through the windows and push in through the ceiling. Tarlow likes to set up comfortable stations for painting and drawing in all parts of the house, including the living room, which is bathed in light from the French windows.

ABOVE The hallway serves as an introduction to the house, including the stairway which reaches up to the guest bedrooms and Tarlow's study. Most of the key rooms, including the master bedroom, are on the ground floor.

ABOVE A spiral staircase found at a Paris flea market ascends from the slate floor of Tarlow's study to a mezzanine bedroom tucked away at the top of the house. The study also serves as a primary studio for Tarlow's artwork and sketching.

Dealing in antiques was Tarlow's first venture when she arrived in California from the East Coast in her twenties. She opened a shop, Tarlow Antiques, trading in collectable pieces mostly sourced in Europe. There was high quality French furniture mixed with Chinese porcelain and Japanese lacquer ware. But it was a difficult market and the dual demands of travelling to Europe and running the business were very involved. She began to move in a different direction, opening her company, Melrose House, in Los Angeles, which represents Tarlow's own furniture designs, as well as her fabrics and wallpapers, with two stores in Los Angeles and showrooms across the States.

"I like to call my furniture 'recreations,'" says Tarlow, "because I recreate a period piece of furniture in my own way and my success in that comes from my background in antiques. Some pieces were more or less authentic reproductions and didn't need to be touched, but with most things I created my own version of it."

As a child, Tarlow never thought that design would become her vocation, despite the beauty of her surroundings. She has particularly fond and vivid memories of her father's house, Windrift, in New Jersey, where she grew up. The large, twenty-bedroomed house was built in 1903 by the ocean, with beautiful grounds. Tarlow attended boarding school, so the house became a focus for her thoughts while she was away, as it was where the family would always come together during the holidays.

But even her schools were bathed in grandeur and elegance. She attended Highland Manor (now Monmouth College), housed in President Wilson's old Summer White House retreat, modelled on Versailles. Later she went to Tuxedo Park School in New York, which was also housed in a striking building. But she always looked forward to returning to Windrift.

"It was beautiful and what I dreamt of when I was away. My father was a big influence on my life, but in terms of design my mother was more influential. She was a wonderful hostess with a very good eye and encouraged me and let me do things she wouldn't let anybody else do. If she had a party I would go and help her arrange things."

But it was only when she moved into her first apartment in New York that she realized how much interior design itself meant to her and that it was a fascination. She studied design for three years in New York, then opened a shop and started on some residential projects. Billy Baldwin was an early influence, but Tarlow has, she says, never stopped studying. Her range of reference is now very broad, although she takes particular inspiration from looking at historical houses, never soaking in the rooms alone, but the architecture as well as the mood and atmosphere evoked by a building.

BELOW The master bedroom lies to one side of the living room. The pine panelling is 18th century, from France, with Rodin watercolours either side of the Regency mirror. The secretaire is English, from the William and Mary period.

With furniture, too, her tastes are wide ranging. Having begun as a Francophile, she also loves Irish and English furniture – spending a lot of time in London, where she also has a house – and furniture from the 1920s as well as modernist pieces. There are few periods she dislikes, but gradually her preference has shifted toward pieces with a certain simplicity and boldness of scale. She dislikes fads and trends, always preferring to steer her own path. In terms of residential commissions, she remains very discerning, having accepted only a handful of jobs during a period of more than a quarter century.

ABOVE The diagonals of a library ladder add a sculptural contrast to the bookcases that are loaded with objets trouvés and books on art and architecture. Each shelf becomes a repository of a collector's passion and knowledge.

"I need to have a project where I really like the client and usually because the client wants to collect antiques," says Tarlow. "I don't see myself as a decorator because I like looking after the architecture and creating the background and then buying the furniture for it. Anytime I have taken a project it's because of my passion for collecting."

Another passion is painting and drawing. Pencils and sketch books sit by almost every chair in her home, and her studio is as much for her artwork as, a place to work on her designs. In 2001 she started building a house for herself in Provence, partly in the hope of devoting more time to her painting.

"We all need to keep on improving and growing," she says, "and there's never a point where you can rest on your laurels. You have to keep going all the time or else stop. And that's not bad either. That's come into my mind many times. One day I will stop all this and have a nice quiet life and let all these new, young designers have their time."

ABOVE The patina of time comes from the use of architectural salvage, such as the 11th-century beams in the living room, sourced in Kent, England, or the quartet of French oak doors. The dark ceilings contrast with the lightness of the rest of the room.

LEFT Sculpted hands sit atop a Henry Moore sketch book from the 1920s in the living room. Books become an intrinsic part of the compositions in the room.

ABOVE The dining room lies between living room and kitchen and has the feel of an old English country house, with its stone flag floors and fireplace. The dresser holds a collection of English pewter chargers and plates with a vase filled with painted tole leaves.

LEFT The kitchen is home to collections of serving ware, platters, baskets and bottles. The fireplace helps warm the room, as does the light pouring in from the garden. English comb-backed chairs sit around the 16th-century folding table.

RIGHT A pine plate rack in one corner of the kitchen is home to pewter plates and Dutch glass bottles. The kitchen was designed around pieces – such as the plate rack – which were incorporated into the fabric of the room.

Thomas Pheasant

IT WAS NEVER REALLY PLANNED THIS WAY. WHEN THOMAS PHEASANT CAME TO PARIS ON A LAST-MINUTE VACATION HE HAD NO THOUGHT OF BUYING AN APARTMENT. BUT PHEASANT AND HIS PARTNER, DANCE IMPRESARIO JUAN CARLOS RINCONES, HAPPENED TO BUMP INTO SOME FRIENDS WHO HAD JUST BOUGHT AN APARTMENT. IT SPARKED AN IDEA. BARELY 24 HOURS LATER PHEASANT AND RINCONES HAD COMMITTED THEMSELVES TO BUYING AND RENOVATING AN APARTMENT OFF THE BOULEVARD SAINT GERMAIN, WITH PICTURE POSTCARD VIEWS OF THE SACRE COEUR AND THE EIFFEL TOWER.

"Sometimes going with your gut feeling is the best thing to do," says Pheasant. "If I had planned it all there would have been an excruciating series of trips looking and analyzing, talking to accountants. I didn't ask too many questions when we found the apartment because I was afraid that I would be talked out of it."

Pheasant spends as much as twenty weeks a year in Paris and it has reinvigorated him and his work. This is the city of Jacques-Emile Ruhlmann and André Arbus, who have long inspired him, while the local galleries and antique shops of the Left Bank had always been a focus for his attention whenever Pheasant visited the city. He has also become the first American to be invited to exhibit his furniture designs at the Pavillon des Antiquaires et des Beaux Arts, held at the Jardin des Tuileries each spring, and has relished the opportunity to establish himself in Paris primarily as a furniture designer, although – perhaps inevitably – he has since accepted an interior design commission in the city.

"I come here and I feel so connected and inspired by French style and history," says Pheasant, "in much the same sort of way that I felt inspired when I first came to Washington. What I was attracted to in Washington were really

OPPOSITE On top of an 18th-century, Qing Dynasty scroll table sits a box by Thomas Pheasant for Baker Furniture. The sofa is also by Pheasant, with a sculpture by America artist Lisa Scheer mounted on the wall behind it.

ABOVE An urn lamp sits on top of a chest by Thomas Pheasant in the entrance hall. Looking through to the hallway, there is an Agostini table with a Colby Caldwell photograph on the wall above it.

ABOVE The light, bright entrance hall was simplified with the removal of closets and clutter. The lacquered commode is a bespoke piece by Thomas Pheasant with the chairs and mirror from his existing furniture line.

classical elements and you see them here on a much bigger scale. It's rejuvenated my excitement in design, and coming here and presenting myself as a furniture designer is very interesting because it's just me, and doesn't require the staff I have in Washington."

Certainly Pheasant's success in the field of furniture design has added an important new dimension to his career. Initially, he began by designing select pieces for individual houses or apartments that he was working on – pieces that drew very much on Pheasant's grounding in neo-classicism but also had a simplicity of line and scale which lent them a sense of modernity, much like his interiors. It was a growing line which could bridge the gap between past and present, at home in either a contemporary home or a more traditional space, and led to the launch of an exclusive Thomas Pheasant Collection.

"As an interior designer I had the good fortune of having clients who were willing to experiment and pay for the privilege. In the process I found a lot of recognition because the furniture became a great vehicle for me, helping me to stand out from the crowd. We did a house project in Washington where we designed 45 unique pieces for a client, which was intense because I have not had that much of a focus on my own designs before and usually we do a few pieces to wed with other collections. But that project pushed me into a position where I was prepared to do the show in Paris and pointed me in a new direction."

Pheasant has also designed a commercial collection for Baker Furniture, updating the more traditional Baker line to attract a new audience, again fusing modern and classical in a combination Pheasant often calls "past present." It's a term that can be applied to furniture or interiors, the origins of his style stemming from a mix of early influences: on the one hand standing in the National Gallery in Washington as a child and looking not so much at the artwork as the neo-classical architecture of the building itself with its symmetry and order; on the other hand being very taken with set designs for films of the 1940s and 1950s, inspired by the glamour of old musicals and Hollywood extravaganzas.

He grew up in Adelphi, Maryland, his father a union arbiter and his mother an accountant. Pheasant studied architecture at the University of Maryland,

ABOVE The fireplace provides a focus for the bedroom, which benefits from light and a view from two sets of windows. Moulding and panelling were restored. The photograph, from 1998, is by Colby Caldwell.

RIGHT The mahogany and glass screen in the dining room is a bespoke piece by Thomas Pheasant. The day bed is also by the designer. Mouldings were restored and the walls painted a neutral shade, which echoes the stonework of neighbouring buildings.

BELOW In the living room the existing fireplace, panelling and bookcases were restored and the green colour scheme replaced with something more subtle. The pair of bronze sconces either side of the window are from the 1950s, by Agostini.

where one of his professors suggested he also take classes in interior design. It was, says Pheasant, as though a light went on and his direction became clear, as he combined architecture and interior design in his studies, forming an architecturally aware approach which has marked his work ever since.

He went to work for Victor Shargai, one of Washington's most successful designers, immersing himself in the city and defining his own approach and style. "When I was studying there was such a modernizing force," he says, "and a push towards architectural minimalism. Even in parts of Washington where there were renovations going on many of them were bold and contemporary, and markedly different from the existing architecture. I was never really very comfortable with that and wanted to really elaborate on the existing vocabulary. That's what people picked up on and part of what I try to do."

BELOW Living room and dining room inter-connect via a set of double doors. When open they allow sunshine to flow right through the apartment creating a great sense of light and space. The existing parquet floors were in good order and restored.

Shortly after launching his own company in 1980, Pheasant bought a house in the Adams Morgan part of the city and renovated it on a limited budget, with a largely monochromatic colour scheme using whites, greys, and blacks. The house was widely published and pushed Pheasant onward. Much of his work has been residential, all over the States, but also in South America and Europe, and in 1997 he was awarded the Andrew Martin International Designer of the Year Award. But as well as houses and apartments, he also worked on the Matisse Café in Washington and the renovation of the Hay-Adams Hotel, and has plans to work on boutique hotels, perhaps beginning with Paris.

He has often been labelled a neutrals neo-classicist, given his own predilection for calm, neutral tones within his own homes, whether it's the Paris apartment – mostly in a biscuit shade, which echoes the stonework of the buildings outside – or his main home, a 1920s gatehouse designed by architect Josephine Wright Chapman.

"I just like calm and personally choose to live that way," Pheasant says, "but I do actually love colour. We recently finished a classical Georgian interior for a client in Washington and the colours are all deep reds and saffron. It's in one colour field and I implemented the same elements that I use in my neutral interiors, mixing different textures and keeping the palette very simple so that the silhouettes and sculptural aspects of the furniture really shine and stand out. Also, Juan Carlos is from Caracas and that relationship has taken me to South America and a totally different environment with all these connections to colour and the passionate use of it. It inspired me very much and now, in 2004, I'm doing red rooms or electric blue."

Whatever the colour choice, Pheasant's work revolves around elaborating upon the existing architecture of a building, correcting and reordering where necessary, and then adding carefully edited and pared-down layers of texture and furniture, with this emphasis upon the sculptural and the dramatic, while also introducing a sense of that 1940s and 1950s glamour through by accentuating fine materials, craftsmanship, and quality.

ABOVE In the bedroom the windows open up to the skyline and create a balcony effect. The room, dominated by Pheasant's own designs, places an emphasis on subtly contrasting textures and tones.

Certainly that was the approach in his Paris apartment, which needed a good deal of restoration before Pheasant could begin to introduce pieces from his own collection, mixed with a few antiques and some designs specially formulated for the new space. It was in bad shape, with the living room – which was painted a rather oppressive muddy green – the only room in decent order. The rest of the apartment had been "butchered," although its potential was clear and its sense of scale and proportion pleasing.

Pheasant spent almost a year renovating the apartment, which is within a building dating back to the early 1800s, renovating or replicating the mouldings and panelling, restoring fireplaces and floors, and hiding pipework and plumbing. The idea was to make the apartment more fluid and cohesive, using mirrored glass doors to help reflect light and open up the space. The results display a typical respect for the existing language and vocabulary of the building, while at the same time Pheasant has introduced a more contemporary and sophisticated aesthetic dimension. "The environment and existing vocabulary are so important," says Pheasant. "One of the great

clues for a designer walking into a client's home is looking for the reasons why they purchased this building, because there has to be a reason. There's usually a romantic connection that tells you a lot about a person. Any purchase I make is definitely a romantic one, as with this apartment. I was looking for something I could connect to and feel comfortable with and there was something about it that fitted in with that. I could appreciate the layout of the space and I loved the light and the views. For me it is like living in a postcard."

ABOVE The neutrality of the colour scheme creates a very calm, contemplative space, which reinforces the sense of tranquillity that comes of the apartment's position at the top of the apartment block.

Joanne de Guardiola

THE 1895 SHINGLE HOUSE IN THE HAMPTONS THAT JOANNE DE GUARDIOLA AND HER FAMILY CALL HOME WAS ORIGINALLY BUILT FOR THE CARNEGIE FAMILY. ANDREW CARNEGIE, THE INDUSTRIALIST AND PHILANTHROPIST, COMMISSIONED THE HOUSE FOR HIS DAUGHTER MARGARET. AND IT WAS A LARGE HOUSE FOR THE HAMPTONS, EVEN BY TODAY'S RISING STANDARDS, WITH TWENTY-THREE ROOMS AND A GRANDEUR SELDOM SEEN IN A BEACH HOUSE.

"It stayed in the Carnegie family until the 1950s," says de Guardiola, "but I don't think the family used it a great deal. It was last redecorated in the 1950s and when we bought it I wanted to preserve the house, but it needed to be updated completely. It was a massive renovation project."

Joanne and Roberto de Guardiola – a Wall Street investment banker – bought the house in 1993. Everything needed doing, from new 50-foot steel beams for resupporting the roof to services and landscaping. Structurally, de Guardiola sought a way to respect the character of the house while opening it up and introducing a greater sense of space and light. Five bedrooms were taken away to create larger spaces and extra bathrooms. A number of windows were also added or enlarged where possible, such as in the dining room where French doors replaced a small bay window. The master bedroom was pushed upward into the attic above to create a dramatic double height space with room enough for a mezzanine gallery, where you can sit and watch the ocean.

"It was a lot of house and a lot of work," says de Guardiola, "and not for the faint-hearted. But really I was attracted by the bones of the house. You walked in the entrance hall, even the way it was, and the bones were

OPPOSITE The fireplace and rug create a sense of welcome within the entrance hall. The classic English country house prints above the fireplace are from the 18th century while the clock is French, as are the two 19th-century armchairs.

fabulous and extraordinary. The proportions are just correct and for a classic, shingle style beach house it really is wonderful. When you are dealing with a structure you have to listen to the way it speaks to you. With a beach house like this I would normally go for a more casual approach yet this house is more formal in its character."

The interiors reflect de Guardiola's passion for updated traditionalism, and free-ranging eclecticism, as well as attention to detail, and an appreciation of light-humoured touches.

Among the most sophisticated spaces in the house stands the dining room, where the walls are coated in iridescent Chinese tea paper – which subtly shifts in colour according to the light – while an 18th-century English bookcase, adapted into a buffet table, sits alongside Venetian mirrors, Chinese dragons from the 1920s, sconces bought in Lyons and a pastel of a North African scene over the mantelpiece.

ABOVE The large living room has a number of seating arrangements, including window seats, creating a good deal of choice within the space. The chair once belonged to Sister Parish.

"I love to mix," says de Guardiola. "And an eclectic mix is what makes a room interesting, fun, and more of a challenge. I like surprises and contrasts, otherwise it can get downright boring. The worst thing you can do is put pieces that are all George III into one room. I would never want to do one period or one country of origin. Even if I have a client who says they just want English furniture, I will try and put in something Continental or something rustic that will add a different texture. And creating those combinations and contrasts is about having a feeling for the right fit. There's something inside you that tells you that's the way to go."

She is always searching for antiques, for work and also for home. De Guardiola mostly buys in France, England, and Italy but has also sourced pieces further afield, in North Africa and Asia. She loves Irish and Russian furniture. She is a collector of contemporary art: Francis Bacon, Robert Motherwell, Jackson Pollock, and Eric Fischl, many of which hang in her Manhattan home. She admires Art Deco, especially Jean-Michel Frank. Other influences include Henri Samuel, Nancy Lancaster, and Alberto Pinto. But in the States her mentors have always been Albert Hadley and Sister Parish. Having arrived in New York and done a stint on Wall Street – which proved a useful immersion

in the world of business – followed by a degree at the Parsons School of Design, de Guardiola went to work at Parish-Hadley for almost eight years. It was a highly formative experience. "No degree was worth two beans if I wasn't going to make it at Parish-Hadley," she says. "It was like an apprenticeship. It was constantly training your eye about what makes something the best, and also learning to take things out of a room, and keep it from going too far. Sister

ABOVE In another corner of the living room, a screen provides an ornate contrast to the neutrality of the background. One of a pair, the Dufour screen dates from 1825 while the armchair in front of it is covered in a Colefax & Fowler fabric.

ABOVE The colour scheme in the living room adopts a soothing palette of yellow, creams and neutrals. The large picture is a Dora Frost pastel which also ties in with the Colefax & Fowler florals of the sofa. The side table is Russian.

Parish would teach us about antiques and expressing your gut reaction instead of talking about provenance and what family owned it in what year. Do you like it and why is it successful? And then it was about absorbing Albert Hadley's brilliance about architecture and balance."

De Guardiola herself grew up in Michigan, the heart of the Mid-West – a rural childhood. Her father was a businessman and entrepreneur, and always encouraged his family to travel and open up their horizons. He wanted his children to understand the USA and took them all over the country on vacations. Even from a young age de Guardiola was reading *Vogue* and following fashion and design with a love of decorating her room or building a treehouse with her little brother. She went to school at Holy Cross, Massachusetts, and then went to New York.

ABOVE LEFT In the living room, a ceramic vase which once belonged to Sister Parish sits on a Thai coffee table in front of the fireplace.

ABOVE RIGHT A mezzanine level in the bedroom creates a look out nest at the top of the house, with sea views. The bedside tables are by Joanne de Guardiola.

ABOVE The library is a smaller and more intimate retreat. The 18th-century round mirror was bought at a Connecticut flea market.

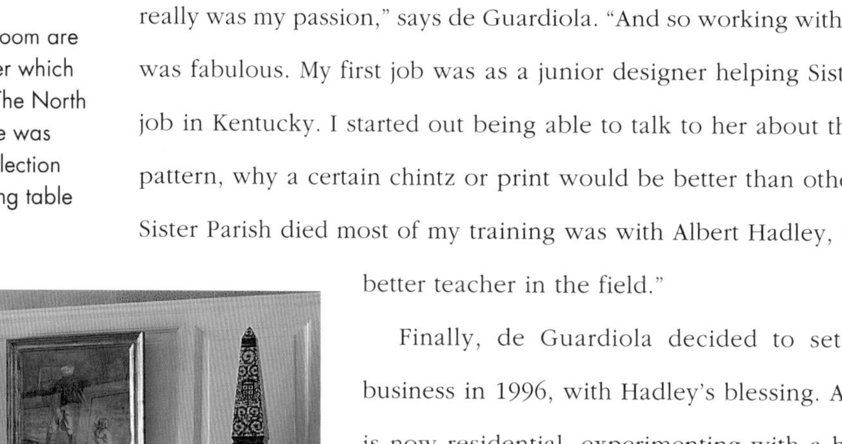

BELOW The walls of the dining room are coated in Chinese silver tea paper which sparkles in evening candlelight. The North African pastel above the fireplace was bought in London, as was the collection of blue-and-white china. The dining table and chairs are Regency.

"I worked in Wall Street for two or three years and then decided that design really was my passion," says de Guardiola. "And so working with Parish-Hadley was fabulous. My first job was as a junior designer helping Sister Parish on a job in Kentucky. I started out being able to talk to her about the rhythm of a pattern, why a certain chintz or print would be better than others. Then after Sister Parish died most of my training was with Albert Hadley, and there's no better teacher in the field."

Finally, de Guardiola decided to set up her own business in 1996, with Hadley's blessing. All of her work is now residential, experimenting with a broad range of themes and ideas, colour choices and textures, from an Art Deco home in Palm Beach in layers of taupes and whites to a New York apartment in deep red and gold, with a good portion of Louis XVI. At the same time she also enjoys working on more contemporary projects, where the interiors are more pared down. But the backbone of her work still lies in many of the lessons provided by the classic English country house.

"It's very important to me that a decorator understands their client and their client's lifestyle and that the personality of the client is imprinted on their home," says de Guardiola. "Within the context of the structure of the house itself, my home in the Hamptons does represent my work but I do also love working in other styles. It's a challenge, which makes it fun."

ABOVE The garden room is a pivotal space connecting hallway and living room. The walls are decorated with a mural by Susan Huggins.

Her home also reveals the importance she places upon humour and accessibility, as well as an element of fantasy. She has a love of chinoiserie and murals, as well as whimsical touches. The garden room of her Hamptons house features a mural by Susan Huggins with painted palm trees and greenery which is echoed by bamboo chairs around a marble-topped table. In her Manhattan home she delights in the unexpected juxtaposition of an 18th-century French tapestry and a painting by Francis Bacon, or 18th-century Chinese panels alongside a Motherwell.

ABOVE The exterior of the 1895 shingle house has changed little, although the interiors and the gardens have been substantially restored and adapted. The barn, now by the pool, was moved across the garden and a lily pond added to the rear.

The garden too has now become a particular focus for de Guardiola's imagination. In the beginning everything had to be levelled and a barn in the grounds – now used for parties and as a children's playroom – moved. She has added the pool, as well as a lily pond outside the French windows of the dining room with a white garden planted around it.

"For me, the garden is a series of outdoor rooms which are evolving all the time," she says. "I still have great plans; across the lawn I'd like a gazebo in a line with the lily pond. But this is a house that is always changing. It's a historically landmarked house and we have tried to stay within the whole nature of the building. But it's also a family house and so it has to evolve. The kids don't quite rollerskate round the house but it gets used."

Mica Ertegün

WHEN DESIGNER MICA ERTEGUN FIRST CAME TO SEE THE SITE IN SOUTHAMPTON WHERE SHE WAS GOING TO BUILD HER COUNTRY HOUSE, IT WAS WINTER AND THERE WAS ICE ON THE NEARBY CREEK. SHE LOOKED ACROSS THE CREEK TOWARD THE BIRD RESERVE ON THE OPPOSITE SIDE, AMONG THE MARSHES. IN THIS CHILLED BUT BEAUTIFUL LANDSCAPE, SHE THOUGHT OF RUSSIA AND DECIDED TO BUILD HER OWN INTERPRETATION OF A RUSSIAN DACHA. THAT'S HOW RUSSIA CAME TO THE HAMPTONS.

"A good friend lent me copies of the Russian equivalent of *Town and Country* magazine from 1911 to 1920," says Ertegün. "I took them home and went through the pages noting everything I liked, deciding on a layout for the house, and we built the house from nothing."

The house Ertegün designed for herself and husband Ahmet, the founder of Atlantic Records, mixes Russian style neo-classicism with a New World taste for crisp and carefully edited interiors. Working with architect Jaquelin Robertson, she designed the house around a large central sitting room, with sweeping views down to the water's edge, the timber dock, and beyond, across the marshes. "The height of this room is wonderful and it is the middle of the house," Ertegün says. "But my husband is a frustrated architect and when I was in Brazil working on a job he decided that the room was too long and narrow and stopped everything. He said he wanted a place to put an orchestra. So we designed an extension to the back of the room, which is more cosy, and it does help. And the views are wonderful."

With fireplaces to either end, stone flag floors, and two sets of double doors to the front entrance hall – where the columns echo those of the portico itself

OPPOSITE The entrance hall is flanked by staircases which ascend to the bedrooms within the two wings of the house. The hallway also leads through to the central double height living room. Along the hall sits a 17th-century Italian refectory table.

ABOVE Fireplaces stand to either side of the living room, with seating areas arranged around each of them. At the centre of the room sits an 18th-century Irish desk. The paintings date from the 1640s and were commissioned by the Austrian ambassador to Turkey.

– the sitting room forms a perfect canvas for Ertegün's concise, elegant compositions. She resists clutter, second-rate furniture, and shabby chic, as well as conventional choices such as "the dining room set." She loves more whimsical examples of English furniture, as well as Irish, and has no qualms about mixing period and contemporary, although her home in New York features more modern pieces than her Hamptons house.

Most of the furniture in the Ertegün's Southampton home was drawn from her own collections that had been accumulated over the years, and placed in storage for professional or personal use. Only the large Irish 18th-century desk in the centre of the sitting room, which was bought in London, was sought out specifically for the house, along with her dining table in the adjoining room. At either end of the living room seating is arranged around the fireplaces, with additional sofas as well as a grand piano in the extra space towards the rear of the room.

The 17th-century paintings of Turkish subjects and scenes, painted by artists in the entourage of the Austrian ambassador, also lend the room an Ottoman flavour. Ahmet Ertegün was born in Turkey, the son of the Turkish ambassador to Paris, London, and Washington. He never lived in Turkey as a child,

moving to the States at a young age, But now the Ertegüns also have a home in Bodrum, designed by Mica Ertegün in traditional Turkish style.

"I first went to Turkey thinking I would use only Turkish things but at that point, in the 1970s, Turkey was not particularly proud of its heritage so it was difficult to find what I wanted," says Ertegün. "I went to the museums and looked at the mosaics, to the bazaar to find Turkish materials to cover my banquettes. I was able to say that I had done a truly Turkish house; I have one table that's English and that's it. Now you can't touch Turkish antiques and they are right to protect them, because they are so beautiful. When you go to

ABOVE A corner of the living room, with an 18th-century Karelian birch settee and 19th-century bergères covered in a fabric from Old World Weavers.

ABOVE LEFT The dining room adjoins the living room and kitchen area. The walls are coated in a tadelakt-inspired pigmented plaster and form a backdrop to a number of Cubist paintings.

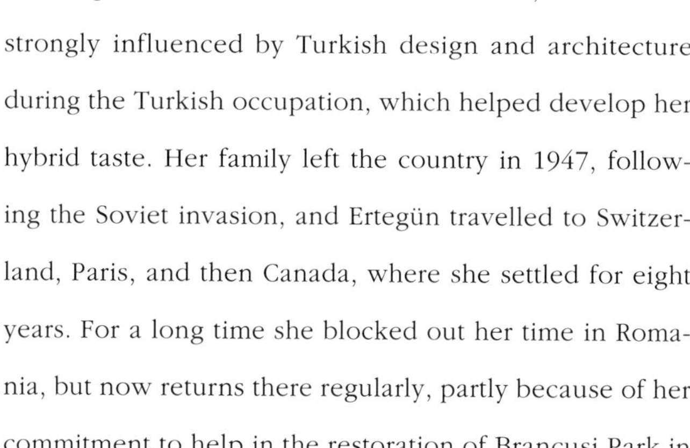

Turkey it's so incredible what you see there: the buildings, the Byzantine architecture. It's wonderful and I was very taken with it."

Ertegün herself was born in Romania, which was strongly influenced by Turkish design and architecture during the Turkish occupation, which helped develop her hybrid taste. Her family left the country in 1947, following the Soviet invasion, and Ertegün travelled to Switzerland, Paris, and then Canada, where she settled for eight years. For a long time she blocked out her time in Romania, but now returns there regularly, partly because of her commitment to help in the restoration of Brancusi Park in Tirgu Jiu – a sculptural complex by Constantin Brancusi, completed in 1937 to honour the dead of the Great War.

TOP A view from the study, looking through the living room to the dining room beyond.

ABOVE A fireplace and seating creates a private space for relaxation and reading within the master bedroom. The icons around the fireplace are a mix of Romanian and Russian images.

OPPOSITE Mica Ertegün's dressing table in the master bedroom, in front of windows overlooking the pool below. The table is draped with Turkish embroidery and holds an Empire mirror.

The first house Ertegün designed was a small farmhouse for herself in Canada, a modest project but one that sparked her interest in design. When she moved to New York, she began by designing her own apartment and then friends began to ask her to work on their homes as well. She decided to study at the New York School of Design.

"I never really felt I would be a designer professionally when I was young," says Ertegün. "I thought I would do it for fun and then I realized that working saves you in New York. Then I met a girl called Chessy Rayner and we became great friends. She was working at *Vogue* for Diana Vreeland and we decided to start a company together. That was really the beginning. We started very small, working out of my home, and then later we needed more space and I was able to buy the house next door. It's very rare to find a friend like Chessy and we never had any kind of misunderstanding. She had a very good sense of colour, having worked in the fashion business, while I was much stricter architecturally. But our taste was always very close."

Billy Baldwin was a good friend of Rayner and an important influence on both Rayner and Ertegün, who called their company Mac II, launching it in 1967. Ertegün also began travelling to Europe more frequently, hunting for

ABOVE The guest bedroom, within the opposite wing of the house to the master suite; the pictures of the four seasons were bought in Lucca. The walls are coated in an Osborne & Little paper.

ABOVE RIGHT A view into the same bedroom is framed by a Turkish portière. The Victorian corner chair is one of a pair.

ABOVE LEFT In this guest bedroom the colour palette offers a strong contrast. Ertegun enjoys experimenting with stronger colours in guest rooms.

antiques, particularly in England and France. She got to know Geoffrey Bennison, David Hicks, and others – relationships that added another dimension to her work and style, which was eclectic and broad-minded, combining elements from different periods and parts of the world, while still being grounded in traditional neo-classicism with a strong emphasis on symmetry, proportion, and the logical flow and layout of a room.

"I don't mind mixing, including contemporary pieces," says Ertegün. "It's like my clothes. I hate to wear an outfit. I buy a blouse, a pair of trousers, something old. Also, I certainly don't like a hundred objects on a table. I'd rather have one strong piece or a good sculpture and keep it simple. And you always have to have a bit of a sense of humour in a house."

Mac II's clients included the late Bill Blass, whom Chessy knew particularly well, given her role as *Vogue*'s fashion editor and her continuing passion for the fashion world and playing her part within it. Ertegün and Rayner worked on two apartments for Blass, as well as his country house. "He was wonderful because his taste was so impeccable," says Ertegün. Following Rayner's death in 1998, Ertegün has continued to run Mac II alone, concentrating mostly on residential work, but also on banks, stores, and other public spaces.

ABOVE Designed in conjunction with architect Jacquelin Robertson, the exterior of the house has the look of a neoclassical Russian dacha that has been transplanted to the Hamptons, and painted in a distinctive saffron shade.

The Hamptons house is suitably reflective of Mac II's style, suggesting the wide frame of reference that Ertegün draws upon. The smooth finishes on the walls were inspired by a trip to Morocco, where she was impressed by the shining surfaces of traditional tadelakt walls – made with a mix of sand and lime and then polished with soap stones until waterproof and lustrous. Ertegün embarked on a complex adventure trying to organize Moroccan craftsmen to come over, until she talked to a local stucco specialist who promised he could reproduce the effect. The colours were specially mixed in with the plaster and the results were just what Ertegün had hoped for.

Certainly Ertegün is not afraid of colour, is prepared to experiment, and is enjoying the resurgence of interest in a more varied palette for interiors. The red guest room is especially seductive, while the coppery greens of the dining room stand out against the honey tones of the sitting room. The Ertegün's own bedroom, in the wing overlooking the pool, mixes icons from Romania and Russia with Turkish fabrics and English and American furniture, part of a suite of rooms that includes dressing rooms, bathrooms, and private study spaces.

Outside, the distinctive long and narrow pool had to be raised up because of the high water table around the house. The whole building is on stilts and protected by a series of pumps against the high tides that occasionally threaten the shoreline of the creek. Ertegün designed the garden with a sense of sculpted simplicity, partly inspired by architect and designer Gae Aulenti's garden for Emilio Pucci.

The scale of both house and garden, mixed with a particular attention to detail and order, makes this a home that stands out among its Hamptons neighbours, in more ways than one. "I wanted the ochre colour when we painted the outside of the house," says Ertegün, "and people said 'but that's not a Southampton colour.' I said 'That's the way I want it.' And now they have got used to it."

Albert Hadley

THE LEADING GENTLEMAN OF AMERICAN INTERIOR DESIGN, HADLEY IS OFTEN LABELLED "THE DEAN" OF THIS CREATIVE WORLD, IN RECOGNITION OF HIS LEARNING AND ERUDITE MANNER, COMBINED WITH A REFRESHING SENSE OF MODESTY AND OPENNESS. PARISH-HADLEY, THE PREEMINENT US DECORATING HOUSE OF THE SECOND HALF OF THE 20TH CENTURY, BECAME A SPECIAL KIND OF GRADUATE SCHOOL FOR MANY OF THE COUNTRY'S MOST CREATIVE CONTEMPORARY DESIGNERS, INCLUDING DAVID EASTON, JOANNE DE GUARDIOLA, MARIETTE HIMES GOMEZ, BUNNY WILLIAMS, AND DAVID KLEINBERG.

Certainly Albert Hadley's working partnership with the late Sister Parish ("Sister" being a nickname awarded as a child which never quite disappeared) – or Mrs Henry Parish II, if you prefer – has to be one of the most fascinating creative relationships of the age. In many respects Hadley and Parish were opposites. Parish was brought up in a privileged high-society New Jersey/New York milieu, and her work was instinctive, creating a powerful version of American elegance founded upon English traditionalism and influenced by the likes of Sibyl Colefax, John Fowler, and Nancy Lancaster.

Hadley grew up in rural Tennessee, but even as a child was looking far beyond the horizon and taking note of what was going on not only in New York, but also in Paris, which was such a creative hub between the wars. He was interested in architecture, fashion, and art and studied in Tennessee and then at the Parsons School of Design in New York. He was open to a wealth of influences and new ideas, admiring Jean-Michel Frank, the Giacomettis and Elsa Schiaparelli, Dali and the surrealists as well as Dorothy Draper and William Pahlmann. Yet Parish and Hadley were a consistently positive, communicative, and productive combination.

OPPOSITE The largest room in Hadley's apartment has been converted from living room to a generously sized study, with the designer's desk bathed in light from the two windows. The sculpture by the window is by Cornelia Kavanagh and the painting by Mark Schurillo.

THE ILLUSTRATED ROOM
PHILLIPS
PHILLIPS
Al and Tipper Gore The Spirit of Family
BARRAGAN
Alberto Giacometti
Bill Blass
LA FOCE

She was a formidable personality, a woman of great style and taste and with a great eye," says Hadley. "We complemented each other. I learned so much from her but I was a little more adventuresome and by that, I mean investigating new techniques and materials that we could bring into the pot. When I joined Sister Parish, her work was purely traditional. It had flair because she had flair and there was nothing pretentious about it. But it was traditional. And little by little I brought a freshness of approach."

One of the first jobs that Hadley was involved in with Sister Parish was a Park Avenue apartment for a young couple. The project was evolving within a traditional direction when the clients declared, while on vacation in Mexico, that they wanted "a floating apartment." Hadley recognized that they meant a more contemporary, open space, which meant reconfiguring the architecture. Hadley worked on opening up the space in dramatic fashion, removing walls and reinventing the layout, while Sister Parish worked on selecting antiques and period furniture and furnishings, which became sculptural against this sleek, new backdrop.

ABOVE The hallway was enlivened by the red walls, rich in texture. This entrance area was simplified and opened out, creating enough room for furniture and closets.

"It was successful and the first major project that we worked on together which was breaking away from the old rules more or less," Hadley says. "From then on we worked very closely together on many projects. My input and her input melded together. We were the greatest of friends and had the most marvellous life together. And I was very fortunate, because I never had to make an effort to get a client. They were just there and the people we were working for were the kinds of people within the sort of situations that I had never dreamed of."

As a young man, Hadley had originally thought he might become an architect. His father owned a company selling farm implements and machinery. His mother was fascinated by "antiquing" and sparked the interest of her son. Hadley describes both his upbringing and family home as very traditional and his parents as supportive of his interests and ambitions, encouraging his drawing lessons and his involvement in theatre. He began studying architecture in Tennessee but decided his maths skills were so "disastrous" that it would present problems if he pursued the profession. Instead, he went to work for A. Herbert Rogers, "one of the best decorators in the south," who worked out of Nashville, an experience that reinforced Hadley's passion for interior design.

During World War II, Hadley was assigned to the Aviation Engineer Battalion, working on the construction of air strips in Europe, including a posting in England. When he returned to the States he enrolled at the Parsons School of Design in New York, where he met the man who was to become a key friend and mentor, Van Day Truex. Truex – who later became design director at Tiffany – was the principal of Parsons and had spent the 1920s and 1930s in Paris during that golden age of fashion and design. He was an inspirational figure.

"He was a very disciplined man and a very attractive man who knew absolutely everybody in Paris at that point," says Hadley. "And the same was true in New York. He had social connections that made it possible for the students to have so-called 'field trips' which gave us access to private houses. It was an experience we had never had before – to see how sophisticated people with real style and taste lived. Mr Truex had a fantastic eye and not only had the educational background but had experienced a lot and he brought that to the students.

BELOW In the study, the bookcases to Hadley's design sit either side of the fireplace. The leather wing chair dates from the 1950s, while the design of the mirror – by Hadley for Baker Furniture – was inspired by a 1930s French design.

RIGHT The living room was unified by the introduction of the built-in sofa. The neutral, stone grey colour tone stands in contrast to the vibrant crimson of the hallway. The mirror helps reflect light and promote a sense of space, despite the limited proportions of the room.

ABOVE A composition to one side of the living room, with a portrait of Elsie de Wolfe and a figurine which once belonged to Van Day Truex.

It was a great period in my life.'" He studied at Parsons for three years and was then offered a teaching post at the school, which he accepted and enjoyed for five years, as well as working as a designer in his own right. Hadley immersed himself in New York, particularly intrigued by the exuberance of those who were stretching the boundaries and exploring the new. There was the energetic imagination of Pahlmann – the head of decorating at Lord & Taylor department store on Fifth Avenue – who promoted flamboyant eclecticism. Then there was the artistry of Dorothy Draper, with her bold use of colour and experiments with scale and theatricality.

Then, in the late 1950s, Hadley was offered a post by Eleanor Brown at McMillen, one of the most successful interiors companies in New York. Brown was a classicist but also interested in new interpretations of traditional ideas and gave Hadley an unusual amount of freedom to explore and develop his thinking. He also gained an understanding of how a business should be run, admiring Brown's acumen – his experience stood him in good stead at Parish-Hadley. He stayed on at McMillen longer than he had intended in order to complete the restoration of Rosedale – a dramatic plantation house in Louisiana that fired his enthusiasm. When the job was over he resigned.

"That night I called Van Day Truex because I wanted him to be the first to know," says Hadley. "He said, 'Do you know who I mean by Sister Parish?' She was just finishing her work at the White House for the Kennedys and winding down. Mr Truex told me she was thinking about giving up the business unless she could find somebody to work with. I called her, made an appointment and had an agreeable meeting. I started work on the 2nd of January, 1962."

ABOVE The study is a place where Hadley likes to sketch and draw within an alternative environment to his office nearby. The sideboard is Hadley's own design with a painting above by a Mexican artist. The standing lamp was bought at the Venice Biennale in the 1950s by Van Day Truex.

One of Hadley's first assignments was helping in the completion of the White House project and later, after the President's death, he helped Jacqueline Kennedy move into an apartment on Fifth Avenue. "She was charming. We used to meet quite often in the street, because I was in my current apartment by then, which isn't far away from Fifth Avenue. One of the last times I saw her she was at the florist's on the corner. She was waiting for something to be packaged and whispered, 'Albert, have you been to the new florist up the street? They are very good and much less expensive.'"

Hadley's own apartment has been through a number of incarnations, changing and evolving over the years. It's in a 1920s building and was largely reconfigured when Hadley first moved in, especially the entrance hall which was opened out and closets added. Later, Hadley redesigned his home again, lightening the colours throughout – apart from the vibrant crimson reds of the hallway – and introducing a number of more contemporary pieces of art and furniture. Importantly, he swapped around his study and sitting room, allowing his work room more space and prominence.

LEFT A slim doorway in the corner of the bedroom opens into the ensuite bathroom. The chair is German, from the 1920s, and the painting by Sugarman.

ABOVE The bookcases add another dimension to the bedroom, offering an additional home to a segment of Hadley's library. The sculpture on the mantelpiece is by Bruno Romeda.

OPPOSITE Splashes of red add colour and contrast to the bedroom. The bed itself was designed by Hadley and the painting above it is by Francis Weinberg. The screen is period Chinese.

"Things come and go," says Hadley. "I'm not awfully attached to personal possessions. There are some things that mean a lot, but I'm usually willing to change if I think of something better. Also place has a lot to do with it. I have a little Victorian cottage in Southport which is much simpler. But in New York, you like to feel you are in town. I'm very attuned to location, light, and space."

As has often been said, Hadley's work – including his own apartment – continues to feel as fresh and innovative as ever. After Sister Parish's death in 1994, Hadley continued to run Parish-Hadley alone but then closed it at the start of the new century, making a fresh start with a far smaller and less demanding office, where he could concentrate on a number of select projects.

"I was not interested so much in breaking the rules as accepting the spirit of the times," says Hadley. "Everything was still based on classical principles. Time has changed attitudes and now I'm working with younger people who know so much more, who are aware of everything, and it has become a more involved procedure. Things have changed. And I can't stop changing things."

fusion

Sills Huniford

"THE GREAT SECRET IN DECORATING," SAYS STEPHEN SILLS OF SILLS HUNIFORD, "LIES IN SELECTING OBJECTS WITHIN A SPACE AND LOOKING AT HOW THEY HARMONIZE WITH ONE ANOTHER. IN THE FINAL ANALYSIS, THAT'S REALLY WHAT DECORATION IS ALL ABOUT." AND STEPHEN SILLS' AND JAMES HUNIFORD'S OWN COUNTRY HOME IN BEDFORD, WESTCHESTER COUNTY, NORTH OF NEW YORK, PROVES THE POINT. IT IS A HYMN TO HARMONY.

Here the furnishing is thoroughly eclectic, the effect melodic and unified. In the living room – bathed in light from six sets of French windows – Egyptian columns mix with chairs by Georges Jacob, a Spanish slate monk's table, a mahogany Directoire chaise longue, an English globe once owned by Rudolf Nureyev, a sofa and ottoman by Sills himself, and art by Cy Twombly and Robert Rauschenberg. Yet there isn't a jolt in this atmospheric, sun-filled room, with its stone flag floors, textured white plaster walls, and marble fireplace. All the more significant given that the house was in such bad shape when Sills and Huniford took it on in the early 1990s.

"It had a wonderful presence about it," says Sills, "but really there was nothing left. The house was totally dilapidated. We kept some of the architectural detailing, some of the original mouldings, but that was about all. We put the stone floors in, the fire surrounds are new, the plasterwork on the walls in there is our creation. We worked real hard at trying to keep a natural feeling to it."

The house dates from the 1920s and was owned by a well-known gardener and author Helen Morgenthau Fox who called the place High and Low Farm. Seventy years later little remained of the gardens, apart from some impressive

OPPOSITE A view from the entrance hall into the living room of the main house. The flagstone floors, the fire surrounds and the plaster work walls are all by Sills Huniford. The columns are Egyptian.

ABOVE The library overlooks the rear garden and functions both as a study and a more intimate sitting and reading room. The desk is 19th-century French. On it sits a glass case containing the wired carapace of a lobster.

specimen trees, and the house and outbuildings were crumbling. Sills and Huniford took their time making their plans for the house and grounds and rebuilt a derelict garage as a guest house – with the feel of a large summer house with strong connections to the grounds and French flavours – which they lived in while they worked on the main building, bit by bit. And the gardens, too, were slowly brought back to life within a series of spaces, secret spots, and a large pool area.

"The house has been like a laboratory for us," says James Huniford, who grew up in New York State, north of Syracuse. "It's what a house should be and where we are most happy. And the landscaping was designed with a modernist sensibility and divided into a series of rooms. A garden should be a journey. My study upstairs overlooks the garden and I spend a lot of time in there working. When I can, I will work from home."

The house sits within a number of key Sills Huniford projects that have introduced a new version of American country to the design world – an original, fresh, modern aesthetic that is contemporary in feel while drawing on period and European references, mixing antiques and recent furniture, as well as modern art, and avoiding chintz and cliché. The architectural background is vital to them, as well as the integration of architectural salvage and hunted treasures, within a collaborative relationship which marries creativity with practicality, originality with resourcefulness.

The architecture has always been an important part of our work," Huniford says. "We have architects working with us on staff and we always find strong architectural elements, whether it's mouldings, fireplace details or columns. There's always that element in our work and I don't think a room can really be successful if the background isn't strong. I suppose there's a element of European design but seen through an American eye – edited and cleaned up. There's an American sensibility to do with function, form, and practicality."

ABOVE The opposite end of the library, with plaster work echoing that in the living room in a house where spaces flow easily into one another. The mirror once belonged to Cecil Beaton, while the table is an 18th-century French wine-tasting piece.

The two started their company in New York in the mid-1980s. Early on, Sills' small apartment was photographed by *World of Interiors* magazine, which led to phone calls from some key clients – who have included, over the years, Tina Turner, Anna Wintour, and Nan Swid – and helped to propel their work forward, much of it residential. James Huniford talks of inspiration from Karl Schinkel and Eileen Gray, as well as the important and influential friendship of Karl Lagerfeld and the supportive, creative relationship with Turner, with whom Sills Huniford worked on a number of projects, including a house in the south of France.

Stephen Sills, who grew up in small-town Oklahoma, was initially fascinated by modernist and contemporary designers such as Gae Aulenti,

Charles Sevigny, and Billy Baldwin, as he studied design at North Texas University. But after college he spent three years living and working in Paris, as an assistant decorative painter to Renzo Mongiardino.

"When I went to Europe it changed my whole thought process and shaped me dramatically," says Sills. 'I started looking at the breadth of architecture and design and pared-down minimalism went out of the door for me. I was looking at 18th-century furniture with a passion. There is a European influence to our work but it's very pared down. Our work is so varied. We don't really have a signature look but there's a thread there to do with a vision coming through about a distillation of objects and how they react to each other.

"There has been a certain simplicity and restraint to our work but now we are creating some projects that are very rich and much more layered. A visit to Russia gave me a whole new idea about the baroque and I wanted to go into that. Our work is always evolving and that's the fun of it: taking different inspirations and reinventing and distilling it into your own creation."

BELOW In the living room sliding glass doors were replaced with sympathetic French windows. The mahogany chaise longues are from the Directoire period, while the two drawings on the wall at the far end of the room are by Cy Twombly.

OPPOSITE & ABOVE The marble columns in the living room were initially not tall enough, so they were cut and slivers of stone placed in between. The apothecary vases sit on a Spanish monk's table in slate with a Robert Rauschenberg painting behind it.

RIGHT A detail of the guest bedroom in the main house. The cabinet is Mexican, in bone and ebony, and dates from the 18th century. The photograph is by Irving Penn.

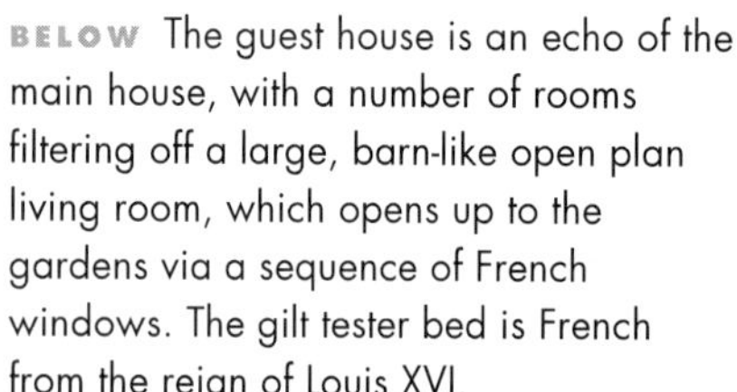

BELOW The guest house is an echo of the main house, with a number of rooms filtering off a large, barn-like open plan living room, which opens up to the gardens via a sequence of French windows. The gilt tester bed is French from the reign of Louis XVI.

The breadth and sophistication of Sills Huniford's interests and references are fuelled by constant buying trips to Europe and beyond. They have worked in France, England, and Switzerland, and across the States, renovating, reinventing, and occasionally building from the ground up. They launched their own line of furniture in 2003, which has broadened the audience for their work.

"We have an incredible partnership in that Stephen can come up with an original idea and I can get it realized," Huniford says. "My ability is to be able to put things together and make them happen and we collaborate on every project. To me, the most successful jobs are where there is a team and more than one pair of eyes."

BELOW The walls of the master bedroom in the main house are painted an earthy shade of green. The steel bed and secretaire between the windows are French. Above the fireplace and John Soane mantlepiece is a congregation of 18th-century Dutch mirrors (just seen).

True of the Bedford house, certainly, which is also constantly changing and evolving – a work in perpetual progress, with plans for a garden pavilion, as well as a new edit of the furniture in the house. It is also a place to indulge Sills' passion for painting: his own work and a modern art collection, represented in the house by Cy Twombly, Agnes Martin, and Robert Rauschenberg.

"Collecting art is a passion," says Sills. "It's the artists I loved as a child and wanted to collect, and as an adult am fortunate to be able to collect. My favourite pieces are the Miró drawings in the dining room. And we add to the furniture every now and then. Change is an important thing in life – not getting stagnant, always editing and changing things and getting a different point of view."

Barbara Barry

BARBARA BARRY HAS CREATED A PERSONAL PHILOSOPHY BASED UPON THE ABILITY OF INTERIOR DESIGN TO TRANSFORM LIVES AND AWAKEN THE SENSES, TO BRING CALM AND TRANQUILITY INTO THE HOMES OF A GENERATION OF PEOPLE ALWAYS RUSHING FROM A TO B. HER INTERIORS ARE SEDUCTIVE AND GLAMOROUS, LOGICAL AND BALANCED, NEUTRAL AND TEXTURED. THEY PAY HOMAGE TO SOPHISTICATE HOLLYWOOD OF THE FORTIES, TO CONTEMPORARY IDEALS OF CONVENIENCE AND QUALITY. HER WORK IS A SYNTHESIS OF A WHOLE RANGE OF INFLUENCES, GATHERED, HONED AND REALIZED WITH PRECISION.

"I am truly and completely an American designer," she says. "I'm irreverent to any particular set of rules or periods, but being an American designer for me means creating a modern synthesis, pulling from everything that has gone before and that is still relevant to today. The glue, or the binding that brings those things together, is naturalness. It's about creating a sense of balance and putting it all together in a natural and easy way."

The focus and drive that Barry brings to her work has led not just to recognition of her work as an interior designer – including the high profile redesign of the Savoy Grill in London and the design of the Boxwood Café at the Berkeley Hotel – but the creation of a whole string of furniture and home accessory collections. There's furniture for Baker and McGuire, fabrics for Kravet, tableware for Baccarat Crystal and Haviland China, and carpets for Tufkenian. There are over a dozen collections in all. Add them together and you have a complete Barbara Barry lifestyle collective.

"I have always had a vision for 'in between' furnishings," she says, "neither traditional nor coldly modern. I started designing furniture for my clients right at the beginning, and designed what I wanted, and found that others want the

OPPOSITE The light of the Hollywood hills throws a soft glow across the living room. Much of the furniture in the room was designed by Barry for Baker Furniture, including the high-back occasional chairs and the Oval X-back chair in mahogany.

ABOVE & RIGHT In the dining room, Barry's Illusion range tea service sits on top of a sideboard by the window. In one corner a Japanese modernist print hangs above an English antique table. The sconce was designed by Barry for Boyd Lighting.

OPPOSITE The mirror helps push light around the room and promotes a sense of space. Barry's own design of dining chairs sit around a Regency dining table, with an English highboy at the far end of the room supporting an Alfred Steiglitz photograph.

same thing. And to me, it's extremely important to be multi-faceted in design because it feeds different parts of you and uses a different muscle. There is decoration in design and design in decoration."

The foundations of Barry's increasingly international working life were laid in California, which is still her homeland, with a house in the Hollywood Hills not far away from her former apartment which is now a "design lab" and offices. She was born in Oakland and grew up in Long Beach, her father worked in insurance and her mother was a painter. Barry's parents divorced when she was nine, creating a great deal of pressure for her mother who worked long hours to raise her four daughters but still managed to be an imaginative home maker.

"She raised four daughters on her own and was also my most vibrant mentor," says Barry. "She was a great woman who taught me that style has nothing to do with money. She was really a closet decorator and so I grew up with decoration around me. She would make magic in the house, coming up

ABOVE Opening out onto the garden, the breakfast room is an intimate retreat neighbouring the kitchen and library. The walls are in a sage green, with French flea market chairs around an English table painted in an ivory gesso.

with colours that she would call these wonderful names like 'elephant's breath green.' She brought imagination and passion to her way of seeing the world and I was imprinted with that from a very early age.'"

Barry attended the Academy of Art in San Francisco, studying art, drawing, and painting. There was also an influential trip to Europe when she was seventeen; France in particular made a dramatic impact upon her, with a way of living and an appreciation of design that helped shape her own approach to interiors. Despite the fusion American nature of her work, French design – particularly of the 1920s and 1930s – has clearly been an inspiration. As well as the influence of Jean-Michel Frank – and his interiors for the Comtesse de Noailles in particular – or Jules-Emile Leleu, she expresses her admiration for contemporary Parisian designers such as Jacques Grange.

Yet, her self-taught aesthetic outlook also draws on the simplicity of Shaker style, the colours of nature and organic textures, the precision of traditional English domesticity, from table linen to fine sheets to taking high tea, Japanese home minimalism, as well as the architectural purity of aspects of modernism. They come together in a personal perspective, simply conveyed.

"Now that I have a body of work I can see that as my education, but I never came at it academically. I feel simplicity is the ultimate discipline. My gods are harmony, balance, proportion, simplicity. I try to create a very tranquil backdrop to the stuff of life – people, clothes, art, books, family, flowers. You can't have too much visual noise so it's about editing and paring down. And my approach to design is intuitive and emotional. I am more interested in what rooms feel like than what they say."

Barry arrived in Los Angeles from Northern California in the late 1980s and started working on a house for cinematographer John Bailey, who encouraged her to immerse herself in design, and then for art collector Janet Karatz, who

ABOVE The guest bedroom has been designed with the feeling of a Parisian hotel, opening onto a separate dressing room, with vintage vellum luggage in view, used for storage. The photograph is by Sally Gall.

asked Barry to work on her New York apartment. It was the beginning of a path that has taken Barry across the States and to London and Japan. Her business includes product design and licensing, residential work and a growing number of restaurants, from The Savoy to a restaurant for chef Michael Mina at the St Francis Hotel in San Francisco.

"I have strived to be articulate so that I could get people to understand where we wanted to go," says Barry. "And it was also about being passionate about design and I think I have been driven. I now know exactly where I am meant to be and I don't care if it's a spoon or a building. It's all about the mixed bag of design, about beauty and function. And now I am very learned – I know where things come from and there's a subtext to everything. But it's still about emotions and emotional responses."

Barry sees her own home as a kind of hotel, looking for the standard of luxury, comfort and elegance one might expect to find there. As a constant traveller, it's important, she says, to have this calm environment to return to, although she calls its style rather more traditional and less strict than spaces she designs for her clients.

The house, built in 1947, was designed by architect Paul Williams. Barry actually first worked on the house for a client and later ended up buying it. It has been painted in a typically muted backdrop of soft colours – parchment, pale greens, and sage – with occasional touches of pattern, such as the Francophile wallpaper by Boussac, lending a Parisian flavour. "Nature is the greatest of painters," says Barry. "I love the greyed-out quality of

RIGHT The master bedroom is a calm space, decorated in a soft palette of creams and natural tones. The English armchair is covered in a chartreuse linen, while the painting on the wall behind is by the Belgian artist Micha Tucek.

things – the palette of taupe, parchment, pewter silver, and then cool blue greens to pond greens. If I'm on a hike in the Santa Monica mountains I'll be saying 'look at that colour,' and then weeks later I'll find it and it will be even better."

This simple, organic backdrop becomes a setting for a mixture of Barry's own designs – with the living room dominated by her pieces for Baker, including her signature Oval X-back chair – together with period pieces, such as the Regency dining table or the vintage French chairs in the library, covered in a linen fern print.

"You can tell from my house that I love having a luxurious, elegant lifestyle but with no particular period," says Barry. "If you talk about what really defines

timelessness it's proportion, clarity of line, the clarity of an idea. These are things unadorned which provide connections through all periods." Fabrics tend to be solid and textured, "like the lining of a jacket." There is no chintz, no heavy pattern books, in Barry's work. She treats a room as a pattern in itself, creating compositions within it, from china tea cups on a sideboard to flowers, an Italian glass lamp, and notebooks on the ivory lacquered desk in her bedroom.

"I do feel as though I'm a painter or an artist creating a composition. But as much as I love composition and beauty I also love the running of a good home. That's something we don't have quite as much knowledge about as the Europeans, perhaps; I know in a past life I was a chambermaid at Versailles, stretching the beds. I'm sure of it. I love to make good homes."

ABOVE The bedroom is generous enough for an ivory lacquered desk of Barry's own design in front of the French windows leading to the balconied terrace. The ottoman in the foreground is by Edward Wormley, from the 1950s.

Vicente Wolf

TRAVEL IS VICENTE WOLF'S INSPIRATION. HE IS AWAY FOR A GOOD FEW MONTHS IN A YEAR, VISITING EUROPE, AFRICA, AND ASIA. IF HE HAD TO PICK A FAVOURITE DESTINATION IT WOULD BE THE HIMALAYAS, BUT WOLF ALSO PROFESSES HIS LOVE FOR THAILAND, BURMA, AND BHUTAN. HE GATHERS NOT ONLY INSPIRATION, BUT ALSO FURNITURE AND SCULPTED OBJECTS, BRINGING THEM BACK TO HIS OWN HOME AND HIS NEARBY STORE, OR TO BE USED AS THE WORDS UPON THE PAGE WITHIN HIS INTERIORS. SHIPMENTS ARE CONSTANTLY COMING IN FROM AROUND THE WORLD.

"It's part of the requirement if you want your spaces to have a very broad sense," says Wolf, at home in his Manhattan loft, on the edge of the Garment District. "I like things that are unique. When you are buying in a city like New York most pieces have been homogenized but I want to look for things that have a twist to them. I look out of the interior design world for inspiration and not having a formal design education gave me the freedom to be attracted by what pleases me. Instinct is my only training."

Wolf was born in Cuba and lived there until he was fifteen. A subtle influence from his childhood and upbringing is apparent in his work: a subliminal attitude which stresses the importance of light, a neutral and fresh tonal palette, and a sense of humour. His parents were involved in the construction business, so he was often around building sites and architects. But in 1961, during the Cuban Revolution, the family moved to Miami, Florida – emigrés who had to leave home and possessions behind.

Wolf lived in Miami for three years, his education still informal, visual, practical, and marked by dyslexia. Then he came to New York to visit a relative and felt immediately at home, soaking in the contents of museums and

OPPOSITE A guest room, lightly partitioned from the rest of the loft apartment, also serves as a more intimate sitting room. The steel framed sofa/day bed was designed by Wolf while the photograph behind is also by the designer.

galleries. There were short-lived jobs in advertising, modelling, acting, and fashion, until he found his direction.

"I came upon the design industry purely by chance," says Wolf. "But once I was aware of it then it all moved very rapidly for me. I started in a showroom, folding samples and sweeping the floor, and progressed from there. Somebody recommended me for my first commission – a midtown apartment – which was published, and from that job came another one. There are very few ways to get into an industry like this and obviously the easiest way is when you know clients socially. But it didn't work that way for me. A great deal has happened through editorial coverage and having my work in different publications."

The designer Bob Patino, who later became Wolf's business partner, was a mentor and guide. They met when Patino was a fabric salesman and Wolf was determined to emulate the path that Patino had set for himself. Wolf even toyed with attending design school but soon walked out after disagreeing with what

BELOW The large open spaces of the apartment's living room have been zoned into a series of areas for sitting, relaxing and dining. The sofa and club chair were designed by Wolf. The table was inspired by Giacometti and to the left is a trompe l'oeil drum doubling as a coffee table.

he was being taught. Instead, Wolf and Patino began working together, in the mid-1970s, and establishing an aesthetic that was eclectic and wide ranging, with an emphasis on architectural background, and a pared-down approach to furnishing and fabrics that emphasized texture and form, particularly influenced by the work of David Hicks and his ability to marry tradition and modernity. They worked together for fifteen years, Wolf continuing alone after Patino's death.

Much of Wolf's work has been residential, but there have also been restaurants, stores, and a hotel, Luxe, in Los Angeles. As ever, Wolf's style is distinguished by its independence, its determination to follow its own path, rather than following fashion. "Following fashion comes from insecurity," Wolf says. "Like a dog you need to lift your leg and pee on the next thing. I don't need to make that statement. My spaces are considered classic in a modern way and they will look good ten years after they've been created. But it's not traditional – it's very much rooted in the present."

ABOVE A Cocteau drawing rests on a French chair in a gallery/library which is to one side of the throughway from sitting room to bedroom. The photograph on the floor is by Richard Avedon.

RIGHT The Swedish folding table at the centre of the room can be used for dining, along with Wolf's archive of chairs. A number of photographs from the designer's collection sit on chairs to one side, including a portrait by Richard Avedon.

Wolf's work has been described as sybaritic – it's elegant but relaxed, working in very mercurial colours, with a blending of different periods and elements, but the result is always a modern environment. And there's a strong sense of architecture. "We do all our own remodelling and have built houses from the ground up. It's a strong marriage of architecture and design. Whatever I produce I try to make sure that it maintains its integrity, a sense of concept and vision."

Wolf's own home is rather less structured than most of his working projects, given that it's in a process of slow but constant change. It's a spacious loft eleven floors up, rich in light and streetscape views – including a view of his office just across the street. Wolf first moved into the 1920s building in the late 1980s, but some years later he was able to buy an adjoining apartment and knock two spaces into one. The transition was seamless, creating a broader canvas for Wolf's collections of furniture, objets and art.

OPPOSITE A 1950s bronze Italian table sits to one side of the library, with the master bedroom beyond. The sofa is 18th-century French with an Italian dining chair in the foreground. The shelves are backed by frosted glass which allows light into the bathroom behind.

BELOW The master bedroom has a natural sense of connection with the rest of the apartment, simply set away to one side, but still benefits from a rank of floor to ceiling windows. A Swedish chair sits by the only windows in the apartment to be curtained.

LEFT The frosted glass wall allows light to percolate through to the bathroom from the windows feeding the library. The table, which forms a home for the stainless steel sink, comes from Burma.

"The first time I entered the space it just felt so New York,' says Wolf. 'It looked like a Woody Allen movie. It was the right space with the right light and the right views. I wanted a loft because I didn't want to live in a conventional apartment. You live in an empty apartment and people say 'When are you going to do it?' but even empty I wanted it to be a space that would satisfy me."

Determined to preserve the quality of rawness and the sense of space, Wolf avoided partitioning or disguising the true flavour of the apartment. Walls were painted white, the floors coated in a reflective super-white deck paint and the banks of windows were left as they were – uncovered apart from the bedroom, which has a need of curtains and blinds. The greatest luxury was the large bathroom and shower room, with a frosted glass wall dividing it off from the library that still allows natural light to filter through. Here a Burmese table was

BELOW By the windows sits a small indoor garden of orchids and blooms, in terracotta pots, on an 18th-century Italian console table. The bedroom has a fluid, informal arrangement dominated by the bed, designed by Wolf.

used as a kind of floating vanity unit to hold the sink, with walls and floors coated in a soothing limestone. Indeed, furniture and artwork throughout seem to float in this gallery-like apartment.

"There are always things that are coming and going," Wolf says. "There's a new favourite and so I fall in love with it and the next trip there's something else. If you have gone through something like Cuba and being a refugee and you lose all your possessions it affects you. After you have satisfied your need for possessions you start to realize that they come and go. First I had to satisfy my desire, which is why I opened a store. I could buy the things that I loved but not necessarily have to live with them."

In the living room, for instance, a Swedish 18th-century folding table is a particular favourite, mixing with a gilded Louis XVI bench, an Eames chair and a sofa and club chair designed by Wolf in one corner. Photographs are one true constant, with Wolf having collected for many years – portraits, hands, nudes, and beach scenes, which are mostly out at Wolf's beach house on Long Island. There's Edward Weston, Martin Munkacsi, Edward Steichen, and Richard Avedon.

Photography has become a passion and something of a parallel career for Wolf. As well as photographing many of his own projects – brought together in his first book, *Learning To See* – he travels with his cameras, taking on assignments. Inevitably, photography has sharpened his eye for composition, as well as increased his appreciation of colour and light. "I know the limitations and possibilities. When you do an interior for a client, your responsibility is to interpret the hopes and desires of your client through your own knowledge and style. But when you are taking photographs it's your own eye selecting what you focus upon, and my photography is always true to my vision without a middle man altering anything. It has put me in touch with who I am as a creative person."

BELOW The bed floats freely in the space, helping to dissolve the regularity of the room. It is anchored by a freestanding three-quarter height wall, which provides a sense of security and enclosure. The photograph on this wall is by Edward Munkacsi.

Mariette Himes Gomez

"I ALWAYS KNEW I WANTED TO BE INVOLVED IN DESIGN," SAYS MARIETTE HIMES GOMEZ. "EVEN AT SCHOOL I DID ALL THE STAGE SETS, THE PROMS – EVERYTHING TO DO WITH DECORATION. I ONCE TURNED THE GYM INTO PARIS FOR A PROM. NOBODY THOUGHT IT COULD BE DONE BUT I GOT A TEAM TOGETHER AND SAID "WE CAN DO THIS." YOU HAVE IT IN YOU. MAYBE SOME DESIGNERS COME TO IT LATER OR FROM A"DIFFERENT DIRECTION, BUT IT WAS ALWAYS IN MY MIND."

Noted for her eclectic, textured, and carefully edited interiors, grounded in symmetry and balance, Himes Gomez grew up in small-town Michigan. Her father and mother – who was a great taste maker, along with Himes Gomez's aunts – both died young. Her mentor figure appeared in the form of Alexander Breckenridge, one of her professors at the New York School of Interior Design, where Himes Gomez went to study after a spell at the Rhode Island School of Design in Providence.

"He was one of the most influential people in my life because he had such a great sense of style and could understand it all," Himes Gomez says. "He tried to transmit that to everyone in his class but for some reason he and I were on the same plane. Everything I do is complex because my taste is so open – I can love a Barnett Newman painting and an 18th-century Italian chair. And Breckenridge was the same. He could appreciate period and historical references and have an appreciation of modernism. He was very open-minded and helped me to open my eyes."

Himes Gomez went on to serve two apprenticeships of a kind in two very different environments. She worked with modernist architect Edward Durrell

OPPOSITE The 19th-century English bookcase, sourced in New York, formed a lynch pin for the design of the living room. It holds part of Mariette Himes Gomez's library and individual treasures and objets d'art. The Persian rug is late 19th century.

Stone and at Parish-Hadley – two contrasting experiences which both informed her work, creating an architecturally-aware approach grounded in a thorough understanding of scale, proportion, and balance. There is an appreciation of context and history, but also a love of surprises and stepping out of context every now and then to bring in layers of other ideas and influences, creating spaces that are uncluttered and distinctly contemporary.

"Every project is different," Himes Gomez believes. "People sometimes presume that I prefer quiet, creamy, luxurious interiors but actually every house is completely different. One might be a rusticated hunting lodge and the next a historic manor house in Ireland. I like that diversity and being able to work on a ranch one day and a New York apartment in 1930s style the next. I don't want to impose my design as an image upon clients. People come and see me and say they can open a magazine and recognize my work, but I don't see it that way."

OPPOSITE Sofas and armchairs lend the dining room an informal and easy atmosphere. The sofa is a bespoke design by Mariette Himes Gomez, while the table was bought at the Sotheby's sale of furniture belonging to the Duke and Duchess of Windsor.

ABOVE The mirror, with a silver leaf frame, dates from the 1930s. The engravings of English country houses which hang nearby were bought in London.

LEFT A view through the pine bookcase, from the living room to the dining room. The dining chairs are Swedish and covered in a damask from Hinson & Company.

BELOW & RIGHT Ceramics grace the mantelpiece of the fireplace, which was already in the apartment, while the painting above is by Carolyn Brady. The mirrors to either side are French, while the coffee table is by Billy Baldwin.

Himes Gomez married an architect, Raymond Gomez, and had two children; her daughter Brooke now works with her mother. She founded Gomez Associates in 1975 and she divided her brownstone townhouse in two with home upstairs and offices below. With her children grown up and a growing work load, Himes Gomez then began to run her life differently with dedicated offices, an apartment in London, which she visits regularly, partly on buying trips, and a house on Long Island. For many years she rented an apartment in New York, but in 1999 decided to look for something more permanent. Himes Gomez made her new home in a 1920s building, within walking distance of her office and reassuringly close to Central Station. She lived in the apartment for a year, planning what to do with it, and then moved out for a time to allow the builders in. Everything was redone, including the bathrooms and kitchen, the floor, and the replastering of the walls, as a calm and considered home came together.

The focus of the living room became a dramatic 19th-century English pine bookcase, which her daughter spotted in a Manhattan antique shop. Himes Gomez adapted the opening to the dining room to accommodate this large unit, with its glass-fronted doors holding a small part of her large library, as well as an intriguing assembly of *objets trouvé*, including Egyptian statuettes and pre-Columbian pots bought in Peru, where Himes Gomez lived for a year with her ex-husband while he was designing and building a hotel in the country.

ABOVE A detail of one of the shelves in the bookcase shows a small composition of Egyptian figurines alongside pre-Columbian pots bought in Peru, where Mariette Himes Gomez lived for a year.

Into the mix comes a Billy Baldwin coffee table, silk taffeta curtains, a Persian rug, an English sofa, and a selection of chairs, mostly French, along with a pair of French mirrors either side of the fireplace. With a passion for symmetry and balance, Himes Gomez usually prefers to couple and pair pieces, while also using furniture to add structure and scale. "If there isn't a symmetrical balance, then there's a balance of some other kind," she says. "I do like pairs of mirrors and objects that have a certain scale, as well

RIGHT The French mirror in the master bathroom dates from the 1930s. The photograph is by Richard Avedon. The unit for the sink was actually a desk, converted to suit.

as surprises of scale. If I walk into any space I can see how it could be improved and see what's going to make it work, such as a large sofa in a smallish room, which I have in my dining room, or how to take advantage of the windows. It's about adding something that gives you a breath of air and excitement."

The dining room was designed not so much as a traditional, formal space but as a multi-functional salon with a large sofa designed by Himes Gomez running along one wall, and engravings of English country houses hanging above. The dining table belonged to the Duke and Duchess of Windsor and was bought at a Sotheby sale, while a Chinese side table sits to one side with a Chinese vase and bowl and a Motherwell drawing. A specially designed unit hides the television.

With regard to the colour choices for the apartment, which she wanted to keep light and clean, Himes Gomez collaborated – as she often does – with architect, colour theorist, and friend Donald Kaufman. The result was a refreshing blush shade, a creamy colour with a flavour of rose. It's just one of a number of working collaborations with architects, including Robert Stern and Centrebrook. "I work with architects a lot because they know I'm going to respect what they are trying to say," says Himes Gomez. "We work with many architects and it's always exciting to immerse yourself in the context of a project. But also I have a design and architecture background. I understand the history of art, home furnishings, and architecture and can put it all together and it will do what it's supposed to do."

In the early 1990s, Himes Gomez expanded her repertoire with a private label furniture collection and more recently began designing a line for the Hickory Chair Company. In 2001, she also opened The Shop in Manhattan, selling a number of her own designs as well as a mix of pieces sourced on trips to England and France. As with her interiors, her store reflects the strong European influence that runs throughout her work.

"I started shopping in Europe during the 1980s," she says. "I always used to think that if I was in New York you could get anything and everything. But now I go to London four or five times a year and the amount of time I have spent in London and Paris has certainly been an influence." She shops everywhere and some years ago she started to buy in Sweden. "I look wherever we need to. I love to look at beautiful things. In London I went to Horace Walpole's Strawberry Hill, a gothic fantasy, and then to a Barnett Newman exhibit at Tate Modern. It was from classic to modern, gothic to minimalism."

ABOVE In the master bedroom the painted and gilded Spanish bed is one of the designer's favourite possessions. The lamps were inspired by Giacometti while the painting of Long Island is by Ben Schonside.

Like her Manhattan apartment, Himes Gomez's Long Island home, in Remsenburg, which features widely in her own book, *Rooms*, also displays her talent for clean eclecticism. Here again there is that great attention to symmetry and scale, but there is far more in the way of colour and pattern in rooms of grander proportions. The backdrops still tend to be muted, but red and rose furnishings warm and enliven the house. The London apartment, in a Victorian building in Chelsea, is more classically English, with many period pieces, while a Syrie Maugham sofa has pride of place in the sitting room. Each is unique, each has its own character and atmosphere. Because, as Himes Gomez says, every house, every project has to be different.

Kathryn Ireland

KATHRYN IRELAND DESIGNS REAL HOMES, WITH CHARACTER AND CHARM, COLOUR AND COHERENCE. THEY ARE NOT SHOWCASES, THEY ARE NEVER PRETENTIOUS OR BRASH. THEY ARE HOMES THAT REALLY GET USED, THAT REFLECT AN ECLECTIC, ROVING EYE THAT FUSES ENGLISH AND FRENCH ELEMENTS, ALONG WITH RATHER MORE FAR-FLUNG ETHNIC REFERENCES FROM INDIA, MOROCCO, AND MEXICO. BUT IRELAND'S ROOMS AND INTERIORS ARE NEVER OVERBEARING OR CLUTTERED. THEY ARE MARKED BY A SENSE OF RESTRAINT, SIMPLICITY, AND COMMON SENSE AS WELL AS ELEGANCE AND WIT.

"What I do is liveable," says Ireland. "I design houses to live in, houses for people who have families, dogs, and regular lives. I don't like anything too fussy or overdone. To me it's quite easy to throw a house together but for a lot of people it's much more difficult. And it's one thing to do a house over the years and slowly put it together, which is what many people do, but when you just want to move in and want everything done then it's a big job."

Ireland learnt her trade by working on her own homes, particularly her house in France, near Toulouse, where she spends the summers, and also her 1920s, Spanish-influenced, hacienda style home in Santa Monica, Los Angeles. She bought her house in France when she 27 years old and planned the complete restoration of the large 19th-century farmhouse, which has steadily evolved over the years, and has included the conversion of single storey out-buildings into a guest lodge.

The house in Santa Monica, along a quiet street lined with columns of palm trees, came along in 1993. "It was in a pretty awful state when I bought it, but I knew it had good bones and I could do something with it," says Ireland. "Before the old garage became a guest house I actually had my office in there.

OPPOSITE The painting over the fireplace was bought from Los Angeles art dealer, Louise Fletcher, who played Nurse Ratchett in *One Flew Over The Cuckoo's Nest*. The candlesticks to either side of it were initially intended for client Steve Martin.

BEVERLY PEPPER
ROBERT DOISNEAU
MANOR HOUSES OF ENGLAND
DESIGNERS AT HOME

ABOVE The arches create a light sense of separation between the key living spaces on the ground floor. The dining room also opens out onto the terraces and pool area. The 1920s dining table was bought in France and the chairs are family pieces, also French.

OPPOSITE A family room lies to one side of the dining area, a place for relaxing, television and music. The pouf was a gift from Shabby Chic founder Rachael Ashley, while the club fenders are English.

I also put the swimming pool in a few years ago, but the rest of the structure is original. This Spanish style is quite common in Los Angeles, with the arched rooms, the stucco plaster walls, and the vaulted ceilings."

Over the years, Ireland opened up the ground floor of the house, introducing arched openings into the family room and kitchen and creating the impression downstairs of one mostly open space, with the lightest sense of separation between the "rooms." A sliding door to the rear terrace, pool, and garden was also added toward the back of the dining area, providing a more fluid relationship between indoors and out. Bathrooms were renovated and

ABOVE The 18th-century copper plated engravings of Jesuit priests were found at an antiques shop in Arundel, Sussex. "I can tell whether there's been a tremor or not by whether they've moved,"says Ireland. The two armchairs were found in France.

the kitchen spruced up with Mexican floor tiles and a few coats of paint for the cabinets. As with so much of her work, Ireland establishes a neutral background – here the creamy off-white walls and painted wooden floors – and then begins adding layers of colour, bit by bit. In the sitting room, the vibrant rug is to Ireland's own design, with cushions on the sofa made from fabric remnants. The two white armchairs were found in France, covered in fabric from Ireland's own collection, mixing with a Balinese day bed used as a coffee table and an English 19th-century bureau, which was a gift from Ireland's mother. Curtain treatments are light and breezy, as befits the climate, but add splashes of brightness in places, such as the dining room where red curtains billow at the thoroughfare to the garden.

"You certainly don't need big, thick interlined curtains here, so what's the point? I believe in doing what's right for wherever you are, not just decorating for the look. I didn't want to leave my background in England behind, but at the same time I wanted to adapt to living here, where there is this indoor/outdoor lifestyle. But I do like a neutral canvas and then layering with colour in fabric, objects, glass, tiles – all those other elements that come into a room. The exception is spare bedrooms where I might have fabric on the walls, as I do here. Some of the houses I'm doing for clients are very large, so I might also do the dining rooms in darker colours, like reds, to make them more conducive to the evenings. At the same time I want to create clean-looking rooms which are not too overpowering."

Bathrooms, too, Ireland prefers to keep simple and decorous. Her own is dominated by a classic cast-iron claw-foot bath, and an oil painting found in a garage sale. Yet, staying upstairs, the master bedroom is far more of a statement, with a grand canopied bed plus a soft Chesterfield sofa adding another level of comfort and indulgence, and mixing with a French table, and bedside lamps made from sections of old balustrade. "I've always liked grand beds where I can pretend I'm the queen when I go to bed at night," says Ireland.

The eclectic nature of Ireland's style and taste partly reflects her background. She was born in Chester, England, and grew up between London, boarding school in Ascot, and a family home in the Scottish borders. The family travelled a great deal which made a big impact, particularly an early trip to Egypt and a number of summers in Florence. "I also remember other people's houses very well and how it used to irritate me if I thought the furniture wasn't in quite the right spot. Rather precociously I'd say 'Do you mind if I move things around?' I always liked houses and was constantly redoing my own bedroom in emerald green or bright red. I loved colour more than anything."

Her only touch of formal training came in the form of a school course in textiles and design, which she enrolled in because she would be the only one in the class and thought her teacher wouldn't bother to show up. But she did

ABOVE The English bureau in the corner of the living room was a gift from Ireland's mother. On it sits a Moroccan vase, bought in France, and a picture of Saint Barts by Louise Fletcher. The gourd was a gift from a friend.

and the two of them spent a lot of time in Peter Jones fabric department, looking at the different weaves and prints.

After school there was a string of jobs, from running a nightclub, to designing clothes, to acting. Having done a spell studying drama early on, Ireland later decided to come to Los Angeles. "When I first came over I wanted to do theatre rather than crack Hollywood," she says. "I thought it was a good place to come and do some training and then go back to England to work. Hollywood as such didn't appeal to me at all. But then I started working with my ex-husband, Gary Weis, who is a film director, producing short films, videos, documentaries. Then I started having children."

ABOVE The bathroom is a hymn to simplicity. Ireland prefers a simple, unfussy and uncluttered bathroom and has a love of old fashioned, Victorian claw-foot baths. The oil painting was found at a garage sale.

Later Ireland turned a small editing room on Main Street in Santa Monica into a shop selling antique textiles, which grew into a store on Montana Avenue. The actor Steve Martin came to dinner one night and admired Ireland's home; Ireland ended up designing three houses for Martin, which was the real beginning of her career as an interior designer. There have been West Coast commissions for actors and directors like Victoria Tennant and Robert Zemeckis, but also work on the East Coast, as well as in France and England. Most of her work has been residential, but there was also the Hotel Oceana in Santa Barbara, as well as suites at the Peninsula Hotel and offices at Universal Studios.

Given her passion for textiles, in 1997 Ireland decided to launch her first fabric collection and the line has gradually expanded ever since, creating a second strand to her business. "My first collection was fairly laid back and I designed it while I was in France," says Ireland. "It really came out of working on that house and was very much a summer house look. Since then I've really enjoyed running it into other areas, woven linens and damasks. But it all coordinates, it's all in the same colour palette. Being an interior designer and then designing a fabric collection I understood all the different colours and textures you might need in a room."

With any Ireland room one comes back to the idea of a real home, grounded in practicality and simplicity. In her philosophy one or two really good pieces will anchor a room. Her preference is for late 18th-century furniture from France or Scandinavia, characterized by its simplicity. She is inspired by the timeless

ABOVE The master bedroom is a place for a more indulgent approach and softer textures. The sofa is an old Chesterfield covered in an Ireland fabric, while the lamps are made from sections of old balustrade.

interiors of David Hicks, Elsie de Wolfe, Syrie Maugham, and Colefax & Fowler. Colour, texture, and layering tie together the many different elements in her work, from North African to French to Scandinavian, without being tempted by fashion statements or passing trends.

"My style is much more European than just English or French," Ireland says. "I think it's a combination of all that travel and love of Indian, Mexican, Moroccan. It's being able to take all those elements and make them work harmoniously together. And doing a room is like being a chef cooking. One too many ingredients and you spoil the whole thing. That's what people find difficult: they don't know when to stop."

Martyn Lawrence-Bullard

MARTYN LAWRENCE-BULLARD'S HOME IN THE HOLLYWOOD HILLS HAS QUITE A PEDIGREE. IT WAS BUILT IN THE 1920S IN MEDITERRANEAN STYLE WITHIN AN ITALIANATE ENCLAVE FAVOURED BY ACTORS, WRITERS, AND ARTISTS; RUDOLF VALENTINO, DOUGLAS FAIRBANKS JUNIOR, AND, MOST FAMOUSLY, GLORIA SWANSON LIVED IN THE HOUSE – NOW KNOWN AS VILLA SWANSON – FOR MANY YEARS, AND WAS LIVING HERE WHEN SHE FILMED SUNSET BOULEVARD. SHE INSTALLED THE ART DECO BATHROOM, WITH AN EXTRA HIGH SINK SO SHE WOULDN'T HAVE TO STRETCH HER BACK.

"I was in New Mexico when I heard the house was coming on the market and we flew back on a Sunday and I immediately called the owners," says the British-born designer. "I went over to see them on Sunday afternoon and within two days had bought the house. I loved it – it's very much the Hollywood interpretation of a Mediterranean villa. But when I bought the house it was very different from the way it looks now. The last person to live here was a Mexican film director who had turned the house into a kind of hacienda with lots of vibrant oranges and turquoise. I wanted to get the house back to those original Mediterranean bones."

The house was protected by a historic preservation listing, so any structural changes needed approval, which meant the restoration took longer than might otherwise be the case. Prizes like the Swanson bathroom and her chandelier in the dining room were left intact, along with Valentino's wall sconces in the hallway. The kitchen is also original, including an arched breakfast nook that Lawrence-Bullard uncovered from beneath layers of plaster and boarding, as well as the 19th-century Italian floor tiles that he found beneath Mexican additions laid on top. The wooden floors were restored and restained,

OPPOSITE The fireplace is 18th-century French, with a pair of early 18th-century ornate Portuguese chairs to either side, which would have been used at a royal wedding. In the foreground Indian ivory boxes sit on the designer's own reinterpretation of a period Portuguese piece.

RIGHT The French doors to the walled garden are framed by billowing silk damask curtains, from Rubelli. The wall sconces are Venetian and in the corner stands a 17th-century Portuguese chest with an Italian portrait above.

ABOVE The chandelier is original to the house, put in by Gloria Swanson, with Turkish incense burners added for a more flamboyant edge. It sits above a Milanese table from the 1880s, while against the wall stands an 18th-century jeweller's cabinet.

the wiring and plumbing redone, the stucco walls repatched and resurfaced, and the gardens relandscaped. In the living room, a mirrored fireplace put in by Faulkner was removed and replaced by a French 18th-century fire surround more suited to the style of the house. The only frustration was being refused permission to unblock a picture window in the sitting room, which had been filled in during the 1940s.

With the bones of the house in good shape, Lawrence-Bullard was free to introduce more of his own character, including a mixture of European antiques – particularly Portuguese – and a blend of period and contemporary artwork and photography.

"I do have a passion for Portuguese furniture," says Lawrence-Bullard, "but really I love anything that has a quirky twist to it, quirky and with a sense of humour. In the dining room and sitting room I've amassed a collection of Milanese ebony and ivory inlaid furniture, some of it 18th-, but mostly 19th-

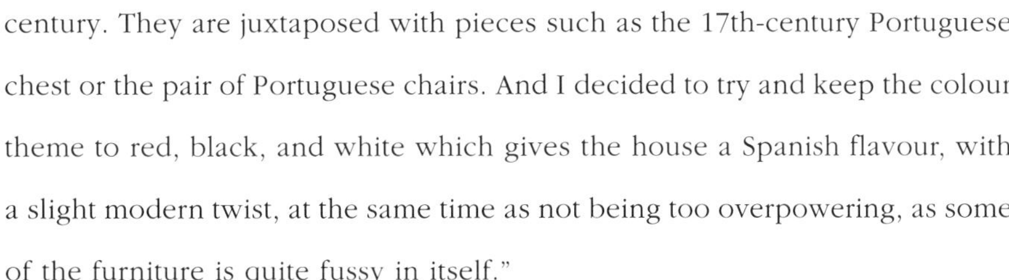

century. They are juxtaposed with pieces such as the 17th-century Portuguese chest or the pair of Portuguese chairs. And I decided to try and keep the colour theme to red, black, and white which gives the house a Spanish flavour, with a slight modern twist, at the same time as not being too overpowering, as some of the furniture is quite fussy in itself."

Antiques have long been a passion. As a child of twelve, Lawrence-Bullard persuaded his father to rent him an antiques stall at Greenwich Market in London, where he would buy and sell at weekends. He began accumulating knowledge and experience, helped by his parents who would take their children travelling a good deal to France, Spain, and Italy, and also further afield, to places like Australia. His mother was Italian and his father Spanish. He was an opera singer in the 1950s and 1960s, as well as an entertainer who appeared in a number of films before becoming a businessman when his voice began to fail.

ABOVE The ceiling of the dining room was painted in a pattern which the designer borrowed from a piece of antique textile. The 19th-century figures are Venetian, as are the tortoise and bronze mirrors.

LEFT The flashes of red in curtains, cushions and upholstery add a sense of glamour to an otherwise black-and-white colour scheme. The circular tables and the club chairs around it are all Lawrence-Bullard's own designs.

ABOVE The library/sitting room on the first floor has more of the flavour of an English gentleman's club. The sofa is Victorian, with small Moroccan and Syrian tables to the side. The photographs of Hollywood stars have personal associations.

Lawrence-Bullard had dreams of following in his father's footsteps, training as a dancer and actor. To support himself through theatre school, including a stint at RADA, he carried on trading in antiques and when he was just 18 was also asked to buy accessories for Ralph Lauren stores – the period props used to liven up the shops. Later, Lawrence-Bullard was offered a part in a television show in Hollywood, followed by some time at the Lee Strasbourg school in the city. He was also offered a part in one of Ed Wood's last films, *I Woke Up Early the Day I Died*, during which he became friends with the film's producer. At a dinner party at Lawrence-Bullard's home, the producer – impressed by the house – asked him to design his new offices on Sunset Boulevard.

That one commission – with a Morocco meets the British Raj treatment – led to Lawrence-Bullard's first residential project, and then a house for model Cheryl Tiegs, a 1950s Bel Air bungalow that was turned into a Balinese pavilion. "Within six months of completion it was in magazines all over the world and really I've never looked back since then," says Lawrence-Bullard. "In a way, it's the Hollywood story in reverse. What's so strange is that as an interior designer you are acting every day because you have to go and put on a show for your clients, so a little bit of theatrics do go into it. I've been offered television shows and parts in movies, which is just extraordinary. I also do television work talking about style and decor, so it's all gone full circle."

Having first arrived in Los Angeles in the early 1990s, a few years later – after his work as a designer had taken off – he joined forces with Trip Haenisch, an American antiques dealer and designer, to create their company Martynus-Tripp. Their client list is suitably Hollywood. For William H. Macy, it was an Arts and Crafts house in the Hollywood Hills. For Edward Norton it was a Mediterranean villa with an English twist. A 1940s Hollywood glamour look was recreated for Christina Aguilera, while Martynus-Tripp designed a Tyrolean mountain retreat in the hills of Malibu for Rebecca Romijn-Stamos.

"The fun thing about being a decorator here in Hollywood is that people have no fear of living out their fantasies and dreams," Lawrence-Bullard says. "I love the diversity of working with these very different people."

BELOW The master bedroom, with its balcony overlooking the garden where Faulkner used to write, is dominated by the 18th-century Portuguese bed. The lamps are made of converted Italian altar candlesticks.

Lawrence-Bullard's work, then, has an element of theatricality and fantasy, drawing on a wide range of references. But it is also built on knowledge and experience, especially of antiques, with regular buying trips in England and Paris, for artwork and furniture. "I love that Oscar Wilde phrase 'all beautiful things belong to the same time.' Here in my living room, on my mantelpiece, I have an Andy Warhol painting, mixed with 17th-century coral, English Pugin Gothic candlesticks, Indian mercury glass witches' balls, and a 16th-century Peruvian mirror frame. There's a spectrum of hundreds of years just there."

As with his home, much of Lawrence-Bullard's work involves contrasts between the simple and the ornate, the discreet and the opulent. Silks are juxtaposed with linens in the sitting room, plain white walls with a patterned ceiling in the dining room, limestone and terracotta with an 18th-century Italian prayer stand in the hall. Upstairs, the library has more of a masculine club feel, with leather sofa, black-and-white photographs, and North African tables. The guest bedroom has a very different feeling – more feminine and more French, with a toile wallpaper and French faux bamboo furniture.

ABOVE Over the original fireplace is a painting of a male slave by Andrea Sacchi with a small Rodin bronze sculpture alongside.

"People on the West Coast rarely use wallpaper, but I love to use it," says Lawrence-Bullard, "particularly in small places like my guest bedroom, which is a fantasy. And in difficult areas I'm drawn to red, which seems to be our colour. I do love using colour, even though in this house I kept the walls in whites, purely because I wanted the contrast between the furnishings and the walls. So many people have been scared of colour for so many years but now we have a reversal going on. Its great to experiment."

Juan Montoya

THE SCOPE AND BREADTH OF JUAN MONTOYA'S WORK IS STRIKING. THERE HAVE BEEN HACIENDAS IN VENEZUELA AND COLOMBIA AND HOUSES IN FLORIDA AND THE DOMINICAN REPUBLIC. THERE ARE APARTMENTS IN PARIS, A PROJECT IN BUENOS AIRES, OFFICES FOR UNIVERSAL STUDIOS IN CALIFORNIA, AS WELL AS COUNTLESS PROJECTS IN NEW YORK STATE, AND THE CITY ITSELF WHERE HIS OFFICE AND HOME ARE BASED. BUT AMONG THE MOST SEDUCTIVE AND NATURAL – EXPRESSING HIS LOVE OF TEXTURE AND ECLECTICISM – IS HIS HIDEAWAY IN THE HILLS OF THE HUDSON RIVER VALLEY.

And it really is a hideaway and haven. The house is set back from the unpaved old Albany post road, a winding track through the trees which once carried carriages from New York to Albany. The house itself is set into a hillside way back from the road, fixed amid 110 acres of land, forest, and mirror surface ponds. It feels remote and relaxed, although just an hour and a half's drive from the city.

"Given that I was born in the country, in the mountains outside Bogota in Colombia, I have always been attracted by nature and I feel the need for it," says Montoya. "For your peace of mind and concentration you need the trees, birds singing. I was shown property in the Hamptons and Connecticut, but I was always drawn back to this area. I was really looking for a place to escape the cement and concrete of New York."

Not that this idyllic spot was free of challenges. The main house, which dates back to the 1940s, was in a very poor state, having been used as a commune. This dark, claustrophobic building required not only renovation but total reinvention, a wholesale reconfiguration that saw a new house emerge from the old. Montoya opened up the building to light and nature, altering

OPPOSITE The library at first floor level flows into the sitting room, with a long balcony overlooking the gardens. The French canvas side chair is 19th century, while its companion opposite is Austrian. The oak bookcases were designed by Montoya.

HENRY V
VANITY FAIR

floor levels, introducing windows, and knocking down walls. A garage at ground floor level was turned into a kitchen and dining room, with terraces beyond the French doors. The main entrance was positioned to the rear, up a flight of stone steps, at second-floor level, with a hallway leading down to a double height living room – where the old ceiling was removed – and an adjoining library, on the first floor. The master bedroom and bathroom were created in the former attic.

"I can't associate the original house with what it is today," Montoya says. "But it had good bones and to build it they had to cut into the mountainside to put in the foundations, which was important. It took two and a half years of work, but that was okay because I was not trying to meet a schedule." The many changes in floor level, partly to do with the fact that the house is built into the hillside, helped in the differentiation of spaces and the creation of more intimate rooms like the study above the library at the front of the house,

RIGHT In the sitting room a 19th-century English screen sits in front of a painting by Eric Hoffman. The Art Deco chairs, upholstered in leather and period tapestry, sit around a table in African hardwood. The steel day bed is 19th-century French.

OPPOSITE The bamboo skin on the ceiling creates an organic, Japanese flavour to the room. The Bakkara rug is 19th century while the sofa from B&B Italia sits next to a wooden centre table from the Philippines.

with a large picture window by the desk giving views out across the gardens and trees. But it also meant that key spaces such as the sitting room and dining room, collared by a timber terrace, could be opened out for balance and contrast and to allow the light to flow and nature to come in.

"I wanted these big spaces with the large window and light coming through. I love the light and if you are in nature you want to see nature. And I spent years thinking about how I wanted the landscape to be and learning about the plants and trees here. You have to learn and make sure that you understand what you are dealing with."

BELOW The dining room is on the ground floor and the granite floors flow out to the cobbled terraces outside. A 19th-century farm table is bordered by American dining chairs from the 1780s. The server was designed by Montoya and the metallic collage is by Peter Clark.

Inside, the house is largely neutral or organic in its colour tones but rich with texture. The bamboo infills between the ceiling beams lend the house a purposefully Japanese quality, but also a suitably bucolic flavour. The floors are in oak, sisal matting, or granite flags down on the ground floor. Curtains are in canvas, chairs are in leather or coated in mattress ticking. The furniture is characteristically masculine, simple, and sculpted, mixing Montoya's own designs with a wide fusion of pieces. In the dining room – one of the simplest yet most elegant rooms in the house – the dining chairs are 18th-century American, mixing with a server to one side by Montoya, Spanish armchairs to the other side, and a rustic American farmstead dining table.

"My work is very tactile," says Montoya. "It's not only visual, it's about touch and the feeling of stone, a piece of furniture or a fabric, as well as mixing elements – the precious and the found. But also it's not static – it's a house that moves a little bit here and there, which makes it more interesting. I love to change and move things, and from the initial concept of the house compared to what it is today, it's totally different."

Beyond the house, Montoya has also added a pool and pool house, while to one side there is a studio with garages below. The studio is almost an echo of the main house, with a similar aesthetic, and was designed as a multi-functional escape – a guest house with its own kitchenette and bathroom, a painting studio, or a depository for an ever accumulating collection of eclectic treasures sourced on Montoya's many travels.

"It's the mix of elements that interests me,' Montoya says. 'I'm attracted to good lines, good craftsmanship and a masculine feeling more than something

ABOVE A detail of a 19th-century weather vane and American Arts and Crafts candle holder in front of a painting by Franco Ciarlo in the dining room. Upstairs, the library holds a collection of antique globes with a Liberty stool in the foreground.

delicate. But it doesn't matter if it's from the 17th century or the 20th century. You can choose a piece by Ruhlmann or a piece by Rateau and it has beauty, finesse, and a sensitivity behind it. Then you can go to Louis XVI and find something very structural and direct. Within the baroque I have found wonderful things . . ."

The studio's suitability for painting has yet to be tested. Early on, Montoya thought he might take up painting as his profession. But he was also training in architecture and design, and design won out. Montoya's grandfather enjoyed painting; his own father was a diplomat who owned a large farm just outside Bogota. As a child, he was impressed by the different homes of his aunts and uncles, while his parents' home housed a collection of European furniture and antiques. His mother and father encouraged him to express himself through design.

"I was always interested in scale," he says. "I remember being ten years old and thinking I'd rather have a high-backed chair in that corner than a low-backed chair. At an early age I was part of how things should be done in the house, which gave me a sense of security and balance. I was adding to my thinking about what I wanted to do and how I wanted to do it and have never been afraid of trying. I'm never afraid of a change."

Montoya studied architecture in Colombia and then moved to America in 1966, attending the Parsons School of Design in New York, where his studies crossed from architecture to decoration and back again and he became enamoured of modernists such as Louis Kahn and Mies van der Rohe. He then moved to Paris for two years, working on his first major residential project, as well as travelling and then spending six months in Italy. There followed a number of different jobs: working on houses in the Caribbean, then commercial work back in New York. In 1978, he began his own company, starting small and building to a string of international commissions, as well as furniture design.

ABOVE The guest bedroom in the main house holds a pair of iron-framed beds designed by Montoya. The campaign desk is Victorian and above hangs an 18th-century painting bought in Morocco.

OPPOSITE A stone's throw from the main house stands a separate guest lodge, with oak floors and beams and calf skins underfoot. The vast painting is by Manolo Valdes and the bed was designed by Montoya.

ABOVE The master bedroom is at the top of the house, within a more intimate, attic-style space. The model boat is 19th century, as is the bronze of Hercules. The table lamp was designed by Juan Montoya.

OPPOSITE The guest lodge is also a repository and sometime staging post for Montoya's eclectic collection of art and antiques. The glass plates are by artist Monica Guggisberg and Philip Baldwin while the ottoman is by Montoya.

To begin with Montoya was considered something of a minimalist, creating pared, down interiors with echoes of the 1920s and 1930s and threads of Art Deco glamour – a sophisticated, urbane look with solid and shining surfaces. But the work has been shifting and diversifying ever since, with more references filtering in, adapting to location and setting, emphasizing texture, function, and simplicity, experimenting with colour and materials.

"It's a combination of a client's needs and the use of a space," says Montoya. "How is a house going to be used? Do they have children? If so, the furniture shouldn't be so delicate that they can't touch it. I recently completed a house in Montana, where the client wanted a place that he could just walk through after riding the horses. The house had to reflect that feeling. Dust is part of it so woods are welcome and heavy comfortable fabrics. It's not Paris."

Montoya's own New York apartment has been through a number of transformations – from ethnic to modern, clean and white. As he says – and as the continuing evolution of his country house also suggests – he is never afraid of change.

"One of the compliments I have had from my clients is that I never repeat myself. It's like being a tailor and making sure that the dimensions and detailing of the clothes you make are perfectly tailored to your clients. And one of the major successes you can have is to reinvent yourself every couple of years, every couple of months. You cannot stay in one place -you have to think of the next step."

Holly Hunt

IT'S HOLLY HUNT'S JOB, SHE HAS DECIDED, TO MAKE INTERIOR DESIGNERS LOOK GOOD. BUT HER INFLUENCE STRETCHES MUCH FURTHER THAN THAT. THROUGH HER FURNITURE SHOWROOMS AND HER OWN DESIGNS, SHE HAS BECOME ONE THE MOST INFLUENTIAL AMERICAN STYLE MAKERS. BASED IN CHICAGO, HER COMPANY CHAMPIONED THE WORK OF FRENCH DESIGNER CHRISTIAN LIAIGRE IN THE STATES. SHE IS SET TO DO THE SAME WITH BELGIAN DESIGNER AXEL VERVOORDT. HER OWN SHOWROOMS AND HER IN-HOUSE COLLECTION KEY INTO THE SHIFTING MOODS OF DESIGN, BUT ARE ALWAYS ONE STEP AHEAD.

"You really do have to be a step ahead, if not two or three," says Hunt. "In a sense we are in the fashion business. You have to smell and see and understand what people want and it has to be fresh. And you have to be able to get in and get out. It sounds as though I'm trading stocks, but I really don't mean it that way. To make interiors and interior designers look good I have to find the best products available, of the highest quality, without being tricky or too terribly trendy, and also provide excellent service."

Hunt bought her first small showroom in the mid 1980s, in Chicago. She represented German-born furniture designer Karl Springer, who was an important influence on Hunt's thinking. She had noticed his work in New York, where she once lived, and where Springer had a store that she would stop by, impressed by the clean modernity of his work, with its echoes of the 1930s. Hunt also began working with Rose Tarlow and Melrose House (see pages 34-43) – a relationship that has carried through continuously. There was a mix of furniture and fabrics, with the blend of traditional design and contemporary pieces shifting over the years. When Hunt met Christian Liaigre in 1992, the company took a distinct step further into modernity. "It has been an important

OPPOSITE The citrine tones of the apartment's grand salon are illuminated by the floor to ceiling windows, with billowing silk curtains. The original chestnut parquet floors were stripped and repolished. The table and chair are by Christian Liaigre.

RIGHT In the petit salon, the small sofa is by designer Christian Astuguevielle, a friend of Holly Hunt who owned the apartment previously. The small antique table inspired one of Hunt's own furniture designs.

ABOVE A detail of a desk top scene to one side of the grand salon. The desk itself is by Christian Liaigre, while the framed drawing sitting on a small stand is by Hans Hoffman.

relationship because it brought something to the market that's fresh and new and created a lot of excitement within the industry," Hunt says. "Interior designers here understood it, even if they were not doing modern, because the proportion and cut and scale were right. It took a while for everybody else to catch up, which gave us a bit of time."

One showroom has become seven, in cities that include New York, Chicago, and Washington DC. Each has been designed by Hunt with a perfectionist's eye, creating environments that are comfortable and accessible as well as suited to the collections she presents. Her own line of furniture – as well as textiles and lighting – seeks to tread its own path, without crossing into the territory laid out by Liaigre or Tarlow, a clean look that updates historical references within a contemporary aesthetic. It's a cross-over range, designed to sit within a broad spectrum of interior spaces.

ABOVE The fireplaces, moulding and panelling are original to the apartment. The standing lamp by the fireplace in the petit salon was a find in an antiques shop on the Left Bank, while the lacquered table and the stools are 19th-century Chinese.

"There's not much that you can't put together if it's designed in the right proportions," says Hunt. "And we are exploring things that other people aren't doing, so we have wonderful forgers, for example, who are making ironwork table bases and we're looking at stone, glass, and parchment tops. There's an emphasis on scale, quality, craftsmanship. American interior designers want the perfect finish and the details to be just right."

Hunt wanted to be a designer from as early as she can remember. It was always there. She grew up in small-town Texas, forever making clothes or moving her room around. She studied English literature, art and design, and fashion, and then started out in retail, eventually moving to New York to work as a jewellery and accessory designer. She began designing interiors for herself and friends in New York and then Chicago, where she started her family, but was always more interested in drawing on both her retail and design experience.

"I've done a couple of interior design projects for other people, but mostly it's for myself," says Hunt. "Interior design for me came out of my love for fashion and design and what you have a passion for you tend to be better at. But I prefer playing at being Ralph Lauren and I have a team, and I get to decide what we're going to make, coming up with ideas. I pick the pieces, the style, the trend. And if it fails it's my fault. But I do feel comfortable taking a little bit of credit for making design showrooms better places, airing them out. I enjoy doing the architecture, and working with the spaces. I'm always trying to get it right and get it better."

Hunt's own homes – which reflect her belief that design is now about a melding of disparate influences across times and cultures, attempting to create a collective resonance that works – are three very different spaces with some common ground between them. In Chicago she lives in a 1914 apartment overlooking Lake Michigan, with a formal quality and a collection of contemporary art. In Aspen, Colorado, she has a new-build lodge for her family, which mixes selected pieces from her stores with more of a rustic flavour, including oriental and Navajo rugs, within a softer and more informal aesthetic. And in Paris, her apartment is very different again.

"If you do have more than one house then they should not be alike. If you are going to be in Paris then have the ballgown silk curtains that go to the floor of the big French windows. But in Chicago, where I have a Great Lake view, I don't even have curtains at the windows. Yet the architectural background is always important and shouldn't be something that you are trying to hide or decorate around. I'm not happy unless the space itself is good."

Hunt took the Louis Philippe (1830–48) apartment on in the mid-1990s. Despite spending regular time in the city, she hadn't anticipated having a home there until one of the Parisian furniture designers that she works with – Christian Astuguevielle – moved from his own apartment to a larger space just downstairs in the same building. He suggested that Hunt might like to take a look at his old apartment. Tempted by the high ceilings, the proportions of the rooms and the character lent by the original panelling, mouldings, and fireplaces, Hunt found herself with an apartment in the eighth arrondisement.

ABOVE & LEFT The simple but elegant kitchen was restored and remodelled by Christian Astuguevielle, who designed the cord coated dresser, as well as the breakfast table and chairs.

Astuguevielle had already done some work on the apartment, which was continued by Hunt. The bathroom was redone and also the dressing room, with its sleek mirrored doors concealing racks of wardrobe space. She asked Astuguevielle to continue working on the kitchen, which has one of the designer's signature cord-covered pieces – a large dresser – against one wall, and he also designed the table and chairs.

ABOVE In the master bedroom, a series of framed photographs of Greek ruins, taken in the 1890s, line the walls. A curtain effect provides a soft backdrop to the bed, while the armchair is by Christian Liaigre.

OPPOSITE The sofa by Astuguevielle in the petit salon sits beneath original panelling and moulding painted in crisp white.

Seldom comfortable living with a wealth of antiques, even in a period apartment, Hunt carried the contemporary stance through into key spaces like the grand salon. The sofa, club chairs, and coffee table are by Vervoordt, many of the other pieces of furniture by Liaigre. "The rooms are beautifully proportioned, and every one has a pair of double windows with a small balcony so you can walk out," says Hunt. "The overall colour is citrine, but there are touches of bronze, white, and brown. You won't see me with a whole lot of primary colours. Softer, more subtle colours are much easier to live with. But it's not about having no colour. You have to have contrast, light and dark, and if it all looks too much the same it doesn't work."

It is an apartment used for business trips, but also for pleasure, visiting with friends perhaps. Hunt finds the Parisian pace more relaxing, less pressured, with more time to appreciate the city, to stay out a little later than she might in Chicago. Yet the calm, composed and restful nature of the apartment makes it a destination in itself.

"There should be a spirit to a room, something intangible that people feel when they walk into a space. The apartment in Paris has that. It's amazing how good people feel when they are in that space. It has a wonderful feeling and that's the secret of truly successful interior design. Not only should it look good, but feel good. Good interior design enhances one's life and makes living better. Then it becomes worthwhile."

contemporary

Karim Rashid

HE IS A RENAISSANCE MAN. A PIONEER OF CONSUMER-FRIENDLY FUTURISM – OFTEN DUBBED AMERICA'S PHILIPPE STARCK – KARIM RASHID DEPLORES SPECIALIZATION AND PIGEON-HOLING. HE IS A MULTI-TASKING WORKAHOLIC, A DESIGNER WHO RANGES FROM PERFUME BOTTLES TO FULL-SCALE HOTELS. HE THINKS LATERALLY AND GLOBALLY AND AT FEARSOME SPEED, CHURNING OUT IDEAS, CHAMPIONING NEW MATERIALS, NEW TECHNOLOGY AND MASS PRODUCTION, LIBERATED BY THE POSSIBILITIES OPENED UP BY HIS COMPUTER, PROMOTING A DISTINCTIVE NEO-ORGANIC, "BLOBIST" AESTHETIC.

Rashid also bathes his work in an erudite philosophy of design, exploring its ability to improve lives and enhance pleasure, to defy rules and borders, to cross disciplines and markets. His freedom of expression knows no bounds, from essays and teaching through to his own book – *I Want to Change The World* – and music, with compilation CDs drawing on his background as a club DJ. He is a renaissance man for the 21st century.

"I made it a mission of mine that I would do what I really want to do in this life," says Rashid. "That's what I've done. I have done clothing, buildings, eyeglasses, watches, shoes, kettles, chairs, lamps, televisions. In a sense it's all part of the built environment.

"And I think speaking about it is critically important. I am a big believer that design should be a global, public subject because everything in our built environment has to be designed. We walk around in various spaces, touch hundreds of things a day, interact with thousands of things, yet there's no discourse about it, nobody knows where these things come from and they take it all for granted. I decided to become very verbose about the subject. I've been to almost every shopping mall in the States talking about it, trying to

OPPOSITE The front lounge space is a laboratory for Rashid's new designs, such as the wallpaper for Wolf Gordon. A pink "Swing" swivel armchair for Frighetto Industrie stands in front of a picture by Rashid's partner, artist Megan Lang.

LEFT By the window sits a small assembly of Rashid's designs, including a "Bloob" stool for Frighetto and a table for Idée. The standing lamp was designed for George Kovacs, while on the window ledge sit Rahid's "5 Senses" vases.

OPPOSITE The front section of the apartment is bathed in light from a quartet of floor-to-ceiling windows with a reflective floor in epoxy resin. In one corner stands Rashid's "DJ Kreemy" fibreglass record deck for Pure Design, underlining the designer's passion for club sounds.

disseminate this idea that design is a way of bringing more pleasure to your life and elevating your experience."

Rashid's New York office, in the Chelsea district of the city, is a hive of activity with products and prototypes all around; at the turn of the century Rashid estimated that he had already designed over 800 products since launching his company in 1993. His apartment, which he shares with his partner, the digital artist Megan Lang, is fortunately not too far away for one so busy. It's just upstairs, in fact – a lab loft also dressed in Rashid's own designs and experiments, from an ergonomic "DJ Kreemy" fibreglass turntable deck to his shocking pink Omni multi-sofa designed for Galerkin.

In the year 2000 Rashid and Lang agreed to ditch all their old possessions – anything bought more than five years before, including Rashid's vinyl music and his books, which went down to the office – and focus on the here and now. They also agreed that for every new addition, something has to go, so

retaining a flavour of fluid, sensual minimalism. The result is that the apartment is always changing, with pieces constantly coming and going, and Rashid always hunting for improvement with an obsessive's eye for detail.

Initially, Rashid wanted a blank canvas to work with, and found it in the form of a hundred-year-old derelict building. The ground floor had been a stable, and the floor above was used for storage; buckets and ropes used for bringing alchohol in and out during Prohibition were found still in place.

"It was great to be able to get into a raw space," says Rashid. "The worst thing is having to gut somebody else's work. That's why we wanted a place like this, although there aren't that many in New York. And we wanted to keep it open because in New York keeping it open plan helps to bring light through

ABOVE The galley kitchen and dining area stand in the dividing ground between the front and rear of the apartment. The bespoke units and dining table are coated in a laminate that Rashid designed for Wolf Gordon.

OPPOSITE The "blobist" painting on canvas, by Rashid, forms a backdrop to a "Limacon" sofa for Idée. The rug was designed for Directional, the chess set for Bozart and the "Bloob" coffee table in the foreground is manufactured by Idée.

ABOVE The separate lounge to the rear is a more intimate space, with a sequence of bathrooms and storage spaces to one side and a window opposite. On a sideboard stands an Ettore Sotsass Memphis lamp. The "Planar" chair was designed for Idée.

the space. One of the hardest things to get in New York is good light."

The bulk of the apartment is one large, long space, running from the front to the back of the building, with the kitchen and dining table in the middle, separating two lounges, one lighter and harder, with a white epoxy floor, and the other softer and more textured, with a pink carpet underfoot, and the large pink ovaloid sofa with glass coffee table at its centre. Only bathroom and bedroom are sectioned off.

Nearly everything in the apartment – with the exception of a desk by film director David Lynch and a sprinkling of Ettore Sotsass Memphis ceramics and lamps – was designed by Rashid, including the wallpaper on one section of the front living room wall, and laminates in the kitchen, coating the dining table and units. Not that it will look this way for long. "Monthly the apartment looks different," says Rashid. "Every Sunday my father used to move all the furniture around in our house and was always rearranging the living room. I think I've picked up that habit."

Rashid's father was Egyptian and his mother British; they met on a Paris metro platform, and Karim was born in Cairo. When he was two years old the family moved to London, where Rashid started school, and five years later they moved again, to Montreal, crossing the Atlantic on board the *Queen Elizabeth*. His father was a set designer who worked for the BBC and then CBC, and was highly creative and inventive.

"My father was a big influence. Painting was his real profession and so we were brought up with brushes and pens and pads. He designed most of the furniture for our house and mixed it with contemporary German and Scandinavian pieces. He would even design dresses for my mother, and he would paint frescoes or cut holes in the walls from one room to another. There was a certain discourse that took place in our family about the physical things in our

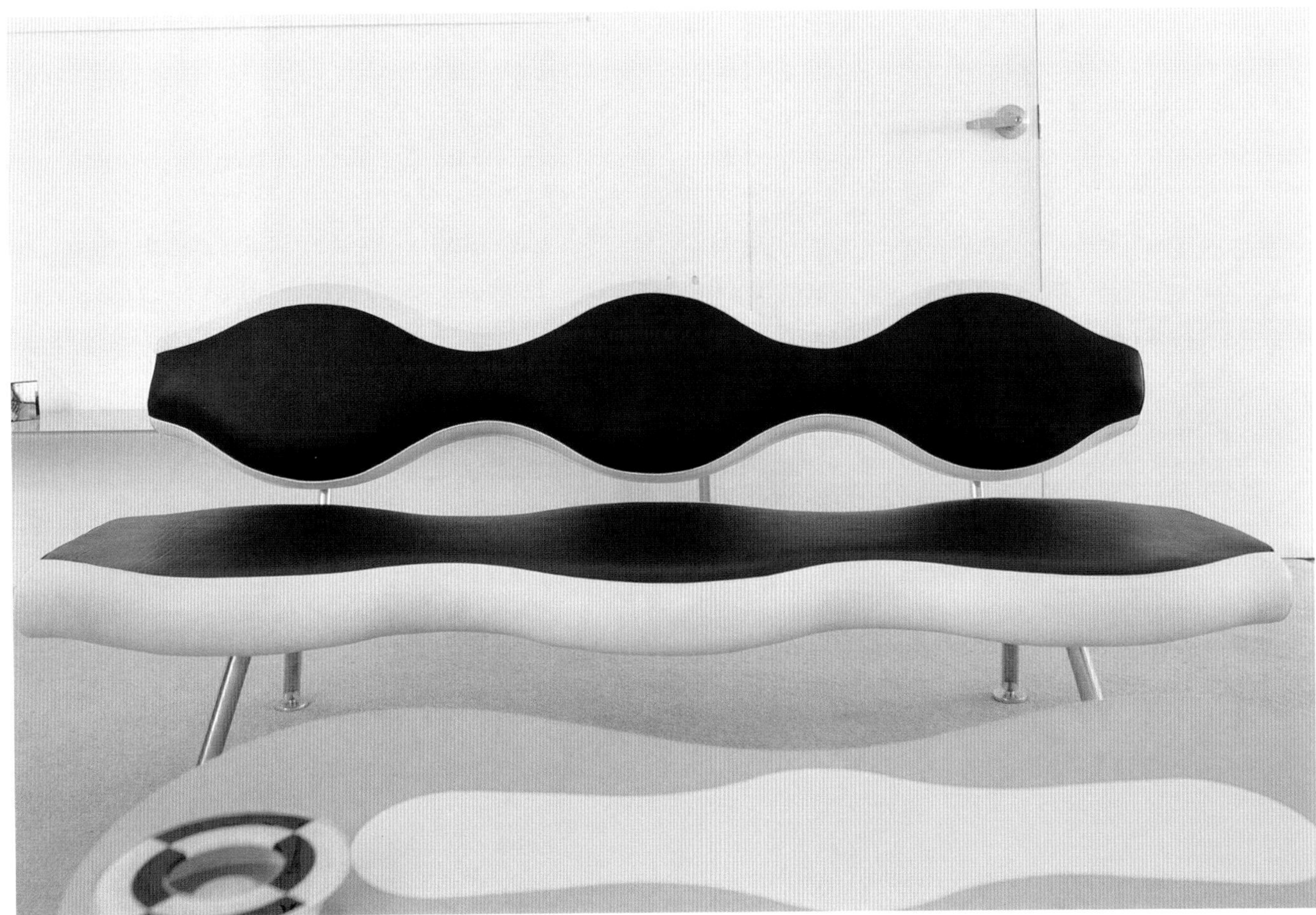

lives. My father would look at brochures for stereos for a year until he committed to buying a Telefunken, and when he got it we studied it all afternoon."

ABOVE The pink carpet softens the mood in this part of the apartment and helps delineate the space within the largely open plan layout. Rashid's "Wavelength" couch is manufactured by Ninekamper while the low table is for Pure Design in Canada.

Rashid went to study industrial design at Carleton University in Ottowa, followed by a graduate course in Massa Lubrense, near Naples, Italy, where Ettore Sottsass was one of the tutors. Sotsass was a major inspiration – as was the Memphis movement – together with Gio Ponti and Italian radical design outfits like Archizoom and Superstudio.

There was a one-year apprenticeship at the Rodolfo Bonetto Industrial Design Studio in Milan, after which Rashid returned to Canada. He then worked at KAN Industrial Designers in Toronto for eight years, designing a whole range of products, from snow shovels for Black and Decker, to laptops for Toshiba, and mailboxes for the Canadian Post Corporation.

"All those years of doing angle grinders and drills really allowed me to express myself later on," Rashid says. "In a way at the time I considered myself an artist

ABOVE The rear lounge is dominated by a dramatic five piece, flexible "Omni" sofa that Rashid designed for Galerkin, with segments that can be reoriented at will. The coffee table is by Zeritalia, with a Bozart toy table (see detail, left) replicating an adult design for Idée.

like my father but to be an artist in industrial design was one of the worst things you could be because it's such a pragmatic field and here you are trying to be artistic. There was no opportunity to be self expressive or reach popular culture. But the world has changed a lot now and I lived through that change."

Deciding that Toronto had become too familiar, Rashid left for the States, tempted by a teaching post at the Rhode Island School of Design in Providence, where he became more interested in the theory and philosophy of design. He went on to the Pratt Institute in New York as a visiting professor. It gave Rashid the introduction he needed to the city – a place he had dreamed of settling as a child – and just enough money to start working from home and launch Karim Rashid Inc. He called or visited one hundred companies and secured just one client. But slowly project followed project and an impetus developed as products began to take off. His low cost, mass-produced Garbo trash can for Umbra has sold over two million and his Oh Chair has also been another major success for them. Other clients and collaborators have included Cappellini, Edra, Bozart, Sony, and Nambé. His work has become truly global, crossing all borders, like Rashid himself who has become a constant traveller.

The step from product design to interiors and architecture came with the Morimoto neo-Japanese restaurant in Philadelphia. Then Rashid began work on a number of large-scale hotel projects, including the Semiramis Hotel in Athens, Greece, where he is responsible for every detail down to the shampoo and music. He was given another hotel project in San Francisco and two hotels for the MyHotel group in England, one in Brighton and the other in Paddington, London.

As with products and furniture, Rashid's interiors strive to be innovative, original, and highly contemporary, experimenting with materials and new technology, but also user – friendly, ergonomic, and experientially rewarding. With hotel rooms, Rashid thinks from the bed outwards, rather than looking initially at architecture, finishes, or location. The room becomes a sum of its memorable parts and parcels of design.

"The interesting thing about design is that you never really know how successful it will be until it's manufactured and physical," says Rashid. "There's a leap of faith that hopefully we are doing something right, whether it's a hotel or a drinking glass. I do know that if I try to deal with as many issues as I can, from economy to quality, comfort and touch, that the chances are the product will be competent enough. But whether it's good enough for people to love you, you just don't know. It's like writing a pop song."

ABOVE The bedroom is a separate space to the very rear of the apartment overlooking a slim courtyard. The panelled "love symbol" artwork is a bespoke piece by Rashid, while he also designed the bed, made by Frighetto.

Lee Mindel

ARCHITECT AND DESIGNER LEE MINDEL MAKES HIS HOME AMONG THE WATER TOWERS AND ROOFTOPS OF NEW YORK. HIS EXTRAORDINARY PENTHOUSE APARTMENT LOOKS OUT OVER A CITYSCAPE OF GLINTING ICONIC SUMMITS, AND ACROSS THE EAST RIVER, AND THE HUDSON. WHETHER OUTSIDE ON THE ROOFTOP GARDEN, OR INSIDE SHELTERED WITHIN BANKS OF GLAZING AND LIGHT, THE CITY BECOMES PART OF MINDEL'S HOME.

"I was looking at another floor in the building and while we were there the agent said, 'The top floor is also available, why don't we take a look?'" says Mindel. "And that was it. I climbed up on the roof and thought this is unbelievable and began to picture it all. Here, you aren't above the view. You are the view."

The form and shape of the water tower atop the 1920s former hat factory became Mindel's inspiration for an abstract rotunda that now emerges out of the roof, and forms a glass living room, and hub for the roof garden, as well as a new partner for the existing functional water steeple. Mindel's abstraction of the rotunda has created a far more complex structure, with cubes and circles intersecting, crowned by a projecting canopy, which owes a passing debt to the crown of the Statue of Liberty.

"Nobody necessarily has to understand that," Mindel says. "But it was a way of thinking about it, and to create a kind of reaching out to the city with this cantilevered crown. But in New York every building's water supply is fed through a tower and it's not until you get up to a place like this and look out that you see them everywhere. So I was looking at the towers and there was this compelling imagery of these beautiful forms."

OPPOSITE The main living spaces of the apartment adopt a fluid, semi-open-plan arrangement, with light delineation around the central staircase. To one side of the dining area is a complementary seating area with pieces by Hans Wegner and a screen by Fornasetti.

ABOVE & ABOVE RIGHT The twisting steel staircase was designed in collaboration with sculptor Larry Wood. It was made in three sections and hoisted in. In combination with a curved wall section and glass screens it helps to partially enclose a reception area under the rotunda, with quartz composite flooring. The double chair is by Frank Gehry.

RIGHT The stairwell is also a lightwell, with the stairs forming a sculpted centrepiece, framed by the glass screens and the line of the ceiling. The chandelier was designed by Syrie Maugham for Lobemeyer.

ABOVE The wooden floors to the main living spaces are in cherry and oak. The dining table is a design by Lee Mindel, while the black leather dining chairs are by Josef Hoffman.

The outline of the rotunda also shifts downward, into the main structure of the apartment below, where its form becomes the delineation of a reception area, partially enclosed by intersected walls, as well as glass screens, and partially open to the main living areas. This singular version of a hallway or vestibule becomes an axis and divider for the broader space, helping separate the main living room at the front, or southern point, of the building from the open-plan dining and relaxation area, as well as the kitchen, behind. A grey, reflective quartz composite floor also helps offset the anteroom, providing a contrast with the cherry and oak wood flooring in the rest of Mindel's home.

A sinuous steel staircase also intersects with the form of the rotunda curling upward and becomes a centre point. It was designed in collaboration with sculptor Larry Wood and hoisted up in sections. "We had to twist it like a vertebrae to get the right approach toward the ceiling," says Mindel. "Within the apartment itself wherever you are there is a sense of enclosure in each space but also the ability to feel the full parameters."

OPPOSITE The main sitting room is to the front of the apartment, with a dramatic view out across the New York skyline. The bookcase is by Charlotte Perriand, the day bed by Poul Kjaerholm, the sofa by B&B Italia and the two armchairs by Mindel.

Characteristically, Mindel has designed a clean, pared-down environment, with plenty of storage – or "shove space" – and discreet areas siphoned off for services and access. Bedrooms, bathrooms, and study are positioned to the rear of the flat, divided within a more enclosed and intimate floor pattern. The palette of colours and materials throughout was intended to echo the character of the city outside with its stone greys and yellow-toned brickwork. The approach to choosing the furniture for the space was – typically again – curatorial and erudite, but with an eye also upon avoiding the feel of a showroom, selecting pieces for their integrity and sculptural prowess. Armchairs, tables, and lamps become a bibliography of the finest designers and architects of the modern movement, with Hans Wegner's Ox Chairs standing out, as well as pieces by Jean Prouvé, Poul Kjaerholm, and Josef Hoffman, plus a number of more contemporary choices from Frank Gehry and Tom Dixon.

These are pieces chosen not simply for their form, but because they have a philosophy of thought behind them, an individuality and sense of separation. "If you value a designer's architecture, their objects and furniture are usually interesting too – a capsule of their voice," Mindel says. "People that have done beautiful work and have a strong philosophy are always interesting to me." They might include Alvar Aalto, Louis Kahn, Arne Jacobsen, and André Dubreuil, but also Palladio, Otto Wagner, and Boullée. The work of Lee Mindel and his business partner Peter Shelton draws on both modernity and tradition,

FAR LEFT & LEFT Carefully selected pieces of furniture become sculpted objects within thoughtful compositions. To the side of the dining area, a Hans Wegner chair sits in front of a Hoffman side table (far left) while an Arne Jacobsen Egg chair (left) sits in the rotunda lounge.

splicing and reinventing disparate inspirations and influences to create something fresh, original, and thoughtful.

Despite his early interest in the visual arts, Mindel originally thought he might go into medicine and began pre-med at the University of Pennsylvania. He was soon distracted by the architecture programme, with which figureheads such as Louis Kahn, Richard Neutra, and Robert Venturi were associated. Bauhaus architects such as Josef Albers were also teaching at Pennsylvania. Mindel switched to architecture and enrolled in a course on the Bauhaus.

"It was an incredible experience," Mindel says. "It was like an architectural boot camp, where you could get your eye to see and appreciate things you usually take for granted. There was something that drew you into it, a power that you didn't even understand at the time or realize what kind of an influence it would have on you. These were the great people of the 20th century."

Mindel and Shelton first met as students at Pennsylvania, although they lost touch and only rekindled their friendship some years later. Mindel finished his studies at Harvard, while Shelton attended the Pratt Institute. After graduating they worked for a number of practices and found one another at the offices of Edward Durrell Stone. For a time they juggled their day jobs with night-time projects, as they began to forge their independence. In 1978, they founded Shelton, Mindel & Associates, beginning with a number of apartments in New York.

ABOVE A chaise longue by Poul Kjaerholm sits to one side of the slim lounge off the dining area. The lamp is by Arteluce. Looking down to the front sitting room, the wall hides service areas and utility rooms.

Since then, their work has spread in many directions. They have worked on the interiors of a German cruise liner, as well as the insides of a jet cabin. Shelton, Mindel designed the Madison Avenue headquarters of Polo/Ralph Lauren and a building for the FILA corporation. They have designed bathroom fittings for Waterworks, lighting for Nessen, and rugs for V'Soske, as well as their own furniture. There have been conversions and new builds, from the highly contemporary to reworkings of period neoclassical farmhouses. Around a third of Shelton, Mindel's work is residential, with a preference for an all-inclusive, collaborative approach to architecture and interiors, creating cohesion and clarity in the work. It's a user-friendly form of contemporary modernism, with a subtlety of approach to materials and colour and a sensitivity to comfort and ergonomics, as well as detailing. "Most of the work that you see is about style, '-isms', and appropriation, and to us that's the most unrewarding kind of work," Mindel says. "We try to do our own work and always try to peel things back to their core elements and understand what makes things tick and work from that. We like projects that we can sink our teeth into, where there are problems to solve and we can use our resources. There's a focus on light, space, and air and working with the site very closely. For us, each discipline is another opportunity to make a project better. The space should be inspiring empty, and then with each step it accelerates to the next level. If we have the opportunity to work on a project in its entirety we like to take it and do the best we can, because the philosophy of the

BELOW A forest of water towers dominate the view from the main sitting room. The black armchairs are by Jules Leleu, while the tall chair is by Poul Henningsen. The rugs are from V'Soske.

RIGHT The master bedroom, with its timber-lined walls, has some of the atmosphere of a ship's cabin. The bed is by Mindel, the chairs by Richard Neutra, while the lamp is manufactured by Arteluce.

LEFT The more private areas of the apartment are contained within a section to the rear of the apartment, which includes bedrooms and study. The bathroom is clean, simple and elegant. The taps were designed by Shelton, Mindel for Waterworks.

space and environment can be seamlessly integrated through the landscape architecture, and interiors."

Mindel's own passion for invention coupled with individuality has been reapplied to his own requirements. He spent many years planning and building a new house on North Sea, Long Island, by the beach. It draws on the vernacular of the area, particularly boat houses and traditional beach homes, with its grid-like cedar cladding, but takes it to a new level of abstraction, juxtaposing the wood with glass and concrete slabs and cracking into the façade of the building to create a more irregular, geometrically complex structure. Again, the design draws on past and present, creating something contemporary and original.

"What I find disturbing about many people who practise architecture and design is that they don't have a reference point. You really have to understand what has come before you and have a sense of discipline, because this is an art form that happens to be in the guise of a service. Often service takes precedence, but ultimately the art can transcend service. It has the potential to become something much better than that."

ABOVE Coloured glass on the window ledge of the main sitting room gives way to the skyline. The design of the rotunda on the roof echoes the water towers. The roof garden alongside includes birch trees in planters, and furniture by Richard Shultz.

Muriel Brandolini

MURIEL BRANDOLINI HAS A TALENT FOR TRANSFORMATION. SHE CAN TAKE A DULL, CURIOUS SPACE AND CREATE SOMETHING RICH, COLOURFUL, AND THEATRICAL. THE FIRST APARTMENT SHE LIVED IN AFTER GETTING MARRIED WAS A RENTAL, WITH PAINTED FAUX MARBLE ON EVERY WALL. SHE WASN'T ALLOWED TO TOUCH THE PAINT WORK SO SHE COATED THE WALLS IN A WEALTH OF FABRICS, CULLED AND CAST OFF, FROM INDIA AND ASIA. IT WAS AN ILLUSION, SAYS BRANDOLINI. BUT IT WORKED AND WAS PHOTOGRAPHED BY A DOZEN MAGAZINES. BRANDOLINI FOUND SHE HAD A CAREER AS AN INTERIOR DESIGNER.

The same was true of her home in the Hamptons. When her husband, Nuno Brandolini d'Adda, an Italian-born banker, bought the 1970s house by the beach, Muriel Brandolini was little impressed by the lack of character within its architecture or interiors. But the house – and a guest lodge some distance away, across the gardens – were soon reinvented with colour, fabric, and playfulness, turning the Brandolini's country home into a warm, exhilarating family space. "It was all about adaptation," says Brandolini. "At least it's so busy now that you don't even see the architecture. And I painted the outside military green, like camouflage, so it disappears into the trees."

The playful theatricality of much of Brandolini's work brings to mind one of the key sources of her inspiration. Venerated Italian set decorator turned interior designer Renzo Mongiardino, who died in 1998, excelled in exuberant illusions, treating homes like stages and using imagination and invention to create exotic fantasies, often based upon modest materials and resources. His talent for recreating period roomscapes, as well as his learning and historical awareness, endeared him to Versace and Valentino and also to Brandolini's mother-in-law, Countess Cristiana Brandolini d'Adda. The Countess and the

OPPOSITE The living room has been transformed by Brandolini's approach to colour, on the walls, in the flooring and furniture. The rug is from Galerie Triff and the sofa by Pierre Charpin. Light floods in from sliding glass doors to the pool terrace.

FOUNTAINS OF ROME
MARK ROTHKO
THE 100
new color new work
ELLE
MAISONS ET JARDINS
ITALY OBSERVED
NEW ART
40

designer became friends, famously working together on a number of homes and apartments, including Vistorta, a mansion house outside Venice.

Brandolini's mother-in-law is the grand-daughter of the Agnelli family patriarch, Giovanni Agnelli, who founded Fiat. Her life rotates from France to Italy to Geneva. It is an extraordinary world. Yet Muriel Brandolini's background also takes in Vietnam and the Caribbean.

She was born in Montpellier, her mother half-French and half-Venezuelan and her father Vietnamese. When she was nine months old the family went to Vietnam. Her father died when Brandolini was a young girl and she, her mother, and her sisters were forced to leave the country in 1972, during the war.

"Even at that very difficult time it was still our country and our home," says Brandolini. "And I am very Vietnamese. If you look at all the houses I have done, in some way they are Asian. There's a freedom to them and a sense of kitsch, but elegant kitsch rather than hippie kitsch, and they are never pretentious."

Being half-Venezuelan, Brandolini's mother decided she wanted to be closer to her father in Caracas. The family settled in Martinique, when Brandolini was

ABOVE A bold horizontal stripe of white, grey and khaki unifies the sitting room, mezzanine study and the stairway, enlivening simple spaces. The large painting is by Jaqueline Humphries, and the chairs by Verner Panton.

LEFT The mezzanine doubles as a study and a more intimate reading room, overlooking the lounge below. The Chinese lanterns were found in Hong Kong.

OPPOSITE The stairwell is lined with period photographs of Venice. Upstairs are two bedrooms and the bathroom, as well as the mezzanine, with a large playroom in the basement.

in her early teens. She disliked her time on the island and reacted against it. She went to Paris for her education, moving from one school to another. Finally, in 1979, she came to New York and knocked on the door of a linen store, asking for a job. "I ended up opening three franchises for them, and created their image. Then I took a year off and Franca Sozzani discovered me. I never really choose the direction in which I'm going. It just happens to me." Sozzani, a magazine editor best known for her work at Italian *Vogue*, enlisted Brandolini as an editor and fashion stylist, and became a mentor figure, encouraging her freedom of expression and spontaneous brand of creativity. There was styling and editing for *Lei*, *Per Lui* and Italian *Vogue* over a period of seven years, working in Milan, but mainly in New York.

ABOVE & OPPOSITE The large painting above the focal fireplace is by Paul Pagk, while the bookcases are by Andrea Branzi. The horizontal stripes of colour on the walls and in the Charpin sofa and artwork creates a sense of thematic, geometric unity.

After marrying Nuno Brandolini and designing their first apartment in the mid-1990s, interior design seemed a perfect fusion of her experience with fabrics, colour, and styling. One client led to others, and she specialized in residential work – large-scale projects which she approaches with energy and passion, as well as the vital ingredient of playfulness. "I like abundance, colour and mixing things up," says Brandolini. "I like to buy in France and Belgium and I love Scandinavian furniture. Every period has something good within it, but I also love contemporary designers such as Marc Newson, Ron Arad, and Mattia Bonetti."

Frustrated by the difficulty of finding the fabrics she wanted to work with, she launched her own collection in 1997, made in Jaipur, "hand-blocked and sun cured." Mostly cottons, with some taffeta and silk, the first collections drew on Indian mughal motifs and designs. Later collections looked further afield,

ABOVE The exuberant throws, pillows and headboards in the bedrooms of the main house are by Muriel Brandolini. The master bedroom has sliding glass doors to a balcony area overlooking the pool.

drawing on inspiration from China, Japan, and North Africa. Later she added a fashion line of djellabas and robes, sold in stores like Neiman Marcus, and Saks.

There was a similar story when it came to paint colours. With strong ideas about what she wanted, depending on light and context, she began mixing her own paint colours, revelling in the inexact science of suitability. "People are trying really hard now with colour and experimenting with it, but they don't know how to use it. My colour choices are totally instinctive, and I never think about things ahead of time, but colour is part of what makes my work attractive. All colours to me are wonderful. They all have a mystery."

Her own homes have been brought alive with colour and fabric. Her Victorian townhouse in New York has a bold red dining room, with Brandolini's Indian fabrics on the walls and ceilings (she has always disliked the coldness of wallpaper), and a Chinese opium bed to one side, while the dining chairs have red velvet seats. The living room is enlivened by blue-green painted walls and a rich choice of ethnic fabrics, with a Chinese silk curtain draped at the doorway, and embroidered slipper chairs around an aubergine velvet sofa.

In the Hamptons, her fearless approach to colour is also apparent. The living room of the main house has been painted in bold, broad horizontal stripes of white, slate and khaki, with white-painted wooden floors. The room is further enriched by a long, caterpillar-like multi-coloured sofa by Pierre Charpin, while a bank of sliding glass doors to the rear open out onto the terrace, pool, and gardens, with a private beach beyond. This abundance of colour is balanced by a sense of elegant simplicity, within an uncluttered arrangement of art and furniture. Within a house lacking in architectural detailing, the bedrooms have also been reinvented with colour and pattern, with striped walls, fluid jigsaw-piece headboards by Brandolini, and her own bright designs for curtains and bed linen.

ABOVE The idea of the horizontal painted stripes is carried through into the bedrooms, including the children's room. It creates a sense of unity to the design of the house, yet variations in colour choices also creates a sense of individuality.

Over in the guest lodge, where the rooms are a little darker, the tone is more opulent. Floors and stairways are painted in reflective shades, while walls and ceilings – even in the bathrooms – are coated in Brandolini's own fabrics. With the addition of Chinese and Asian artwork and furniture, the effect is contemporary ethnic, filtered through a fresh eye.

As well as Mongiardino, Brandolini's other great influence and inspiration is David Hicks. Hicks was famous for his unabashed and eclectic use of colour, building on the traditions and themes of the past. Brandolini's increasingly sophisticated and exuberant use of colour and pattern stands out all the more in a world still tempted towards conservatism and the safety of the beige and the bland.

LEFT This bedroom in the guest cottage is lent a sumptuous atmosphere by a four-poster bed with a floating fabric net designed by Brandolini. The floors are painted in a contrasting, rich turquoise shade.

BELOW Brandolini's fabrics enliven the interior of the guest cottage and cover almost every wall in the house, including the bathrooms. Here the choice of furniture and colours lends this guest bedroom an Oriental theme.

ABOVE The conservatory in the main house functions as a secondary sitting room, as well as a dining room. The rug is Tunisian while the chairs are by Marc Newson. Blinds help filter the heat in the summer months.

Tsao & McKown

THEY ARE GREAT COLLECTORS, ZACK MCKOWN AND CALVIN TSAO. GIVEN THE SOFT, REFINED APPROACH TO MINIMALISM, YOU MIGHT NOT GUESS IT. AMONG THEIR OWN FURNITURE DESIGNS AND COUNTLESS ELEMENTS OF THE BESPOKE, THERE ARE A GOOD CHOICE OF STRUCTURED, MASCULINE PERIOD PIECES. BUT STILL, THE OVERALL EFFECT IS ONE OF COMPOSED MODERNITY. YET OPEN ANY OF THE BANKS OF CUPBOARDS WHICH LINE THE APARTMENT, AND RACK UPON RACK OF TREASURES STARE BACK AT YOU: CHINA AND CERAMICS, POTS AND PANS, CURIOS, AS WELL AS A LIBRARY OF BOOKS.

"I love collecting things from the early industrial age, when engineers especially were designing parts of machines, and other things for utilitarian use, with an almost subconscious and very strong sense of aesthetics and crafts," says McKown. "So even though they are supposed to be utilitarian they end up being quite beautiful. There's a purity to it and a certain humility. It's not about the designer's statement but immersing thought in what this thing needs to be."

Their approach to such finds, says Tsao and McKown, is quintessentially Japanese. In their home they take things out and enjoy them, as and when they want, and then put them away again. So the apartment is never frozen in time; it's always subtly shifting and changing, but also peaceful, and uncluttered.

"We believe that an interior should never be a museum or a frozen environment," Tsao says. "A successful design is one that provides you with all the ingredients that allow you to live fully, and to grow, and evolve. In that sense our apartment is very relevant to our work. There are things we might revisit but on a fundamental level it reflects what we do in terms of light, colour, and natural conditions. And we still firmly believe that you don't need unnecessary embellishment."

OPPOSITE The dining area sits to one side of the open plan living spaces on the lower floor of the apartment. The dining table, in cherry, was designed by Tsao-McKown, while the dining chairs are 18th-century Scottish. The candlesticks are American, from the 1940s.

Tsao and McKown bought the apartment, overlooking Central Park and the Natural History Museum, in 1995. They wanted southern light, a park view – which they also had with their previous home – and space. They liked the fact that the duplex, within a 1930s building, had four discernible corners that lent the apartment some of the feeling of a house, and at 3,500 square feet it certainly had space. The apartment had also been renovated many times over the years, with little left of the original features, and a mess of styles. This gave Tsao and McKown ready freedom to completely reinvent the space, opening it up and creating a more fluid, open environment.

Originally the apartment was divided into a series of rooms, with the staircase discreet and unspectacular. Tsao and McKown created a largely open plan space on the lower floor of the apartment, with Brazilian cherry wood floors, and a dramatic, sculpted spiral staircase at the centre of this large room, partially dividing the kitchen from the key seating and dining area, which has a series of south-facing windows. Only the services are separated off, with a utility room to the rear of the kitchen, while upstairs there is a more familiar division of spaces into a series of bedrooms and bathrooms.

ABOVE A detail of the entrance area, which flows into the open plan arrangement of the main living space. The photograph is by Adam Fuss, while a Swedish vase from the 1930s sits on the side table.

"The staircase was an opportunity to do something sculptural, which was a pleasure," says McKown. "Most of the architectural vocabulary was meant to recede so you are not really aware of it – to feel it, but not to notice it right away. With the stairs, on the other hand, it's okay to notice it. That's part of its function. Here we really took the opportunity to experiment upon ourselves. Practically everything is custom-designed. We even went so far as to redesign the front and side of the cooking range. And here we did what we often do, which is using pieces of furniture that we find beautiful or interesting and then designing extra pieces to complete the composition and provide comfort, such as the big sofa, coffee table, and dining table."

The apartment, like so much of their work, was a truly collaborative process. Having known one another since university, Tsao and McKown have a great deal of shared history and understanding to draw upon. Tsao prefers to cast the net wide and consider all the possibilities within a project, firing ideas into the mix. McKown is the one who finds the essence of a job, editing these ideas

ABOVE The silver-leafed cupboards along the wall and above the fireplace hold bookshelves and other collections. The day bed is a flea market find, as was the 19th-century hospital tray table, found in Paris.

down to their essential core. "At the end of the day we are born of the same stuff, and so in the end we will always agree on what's right, and what's wrong," Tsao says. "And we do actually work together. There are many partnerships where one person is doing this job and the other is doing that. But we have different strengths, which we want to bring to the same projects, and also make sure that our weaknesses are under check."

And yet their backgrounds are very different. Calvin Tsao's family is from Shanghai, but moved to Hong Kong, where Tsao was born. Then there was time in Singapore and Malaysia before the family finally settled in California, when Tsao was a teenager and thrown into a very different "Brady Bunch"

ABOVE The curving sculpted staircase helps to lightly divide or zone the main living areas within an open-plan arrangement. The cross on the wall is Sicilian, bought in London.

BELOW A breakfast area sits to the side of the kitchen on the lower floor. The table is originally a piece of garden furniture, bought at the Paris flea market, while the chairs are by André Arbus.

world, having soaked in the influences, colours, and textures of Asia. He decided to study to be an actor, in Pittsburgh, and also tried his hand at directing, before deciding it just wasn't right for him. He moved to Harvard to study architecture, where he first met Zack McKown, followed by a year working with Richard Meier and seven years with I.M. Pei.

"It's the combination of those two work experiences that has a certain influence," says Tsao. "Meier has evolved an amazing language and vocabulary and has the discipline of sticking to an identity. With Pei, it was about judgement. He really understood his place and architecture's place in society and history, and its place in the physical landscape, and the built environment."

With Pei, Tsao returned to Asia, working on the Fragrant Hills hotel in Beijing, China and then – more importantly, the Bank of China Tower in Hong Kong. When Tsao & McKown was established in 1985, among the company's first projects were a high rise building in Shanghai and Suntec City in Singapore – a million-square-foot complex including office towers and a convention centre.

Zack McKown grew up in South Carolina. His mother was a painter and amateur architect, who renovated the family home in the manner of Frank Lloyd Wright. There was an influential trip to Europe, while he was still at college, where he was deeply impressed by Palladio's work, particularly the first of Palladio's houses he ever saw – La Malcontenta.

"Our work is grounded in classicism," says McKown. "Modernism is grounded in classicism, although the modern movement, like so many revolutions, inadvertently killed off, for a time, much that was good at the same time as trying to reawaken people. We see ourselves as modernists and classicists and don't see that as contradictory."

There was also the important influence of Louis Kahn and Le Corbusier. McKown went to Harvard, then worked with Rafael Viñoly – the Uruguayan born architect – in his New York office. And since they began working together, McKown and Tsao have, crucially, adopted a broad approach to the work they commit to, fusing architecture and interiors, but also encompassing exhibition and product design. As well as many houses and apartments, there have been restaurants and hotels, including the Wheatleigh Hotel in Massachusetts, rooms

ABOVE The curving underside of the staircase frames the view toward the front of the apartment, with its sequence of windows throwing light across the Brazilian cherry wood floors. The two early 19th-century French Masonic stools were bought at the Galerie Camoin in Paris.

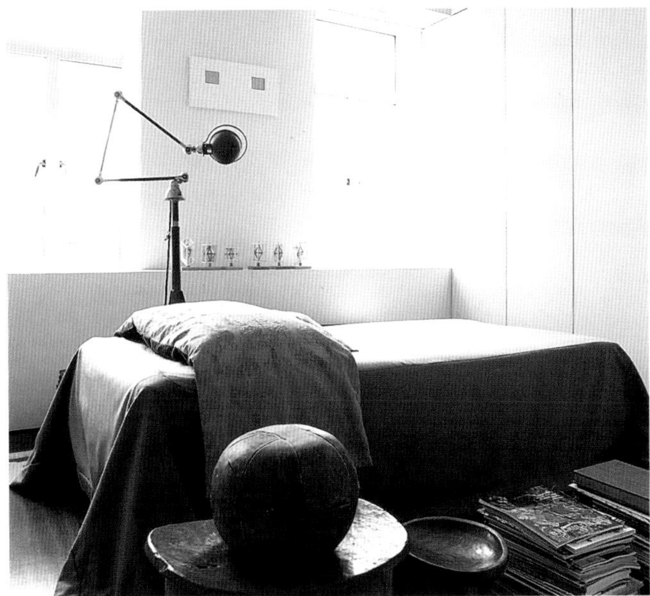

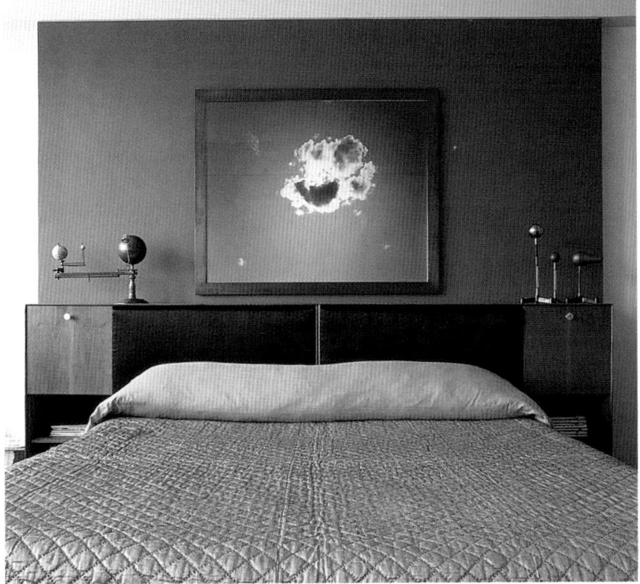

at the Tribeca Grand in New York, and a boutique hotel in Berlin. There has been the renovation of a 1930s block in Soho into apartments and also work on a new build apartment block in Tribeca – their first new building in the city.

"It's extremely important that we understand the cultures that we are working in and even though Calvin has a Chinese background, it's our own back yard that we understand the best," says McKown. "There are times that we do have opportunities in Europe, and then part of the pleasure is a self-immersion in that culture, trying to understand as much as we can."

'We have sought to do a wide range of projects, many building types as well as interiors, and even when we work on the same sort of building again, we always try to make it a new project, and review all the parameters afresh. And when it came to the interior of our buildings we saw that we had better do them ourselves if we wanted the buildings to be finished well. So we are always thinking about the smallest aspects of the interior from the beginning. If one doesn't get to complete the interior of a project, it's almost like an amputation."

Certainly the attention to detail in their work, from their own apartment to apartment buildings, is quite extraordinary. It is spliced with originality and invention, making Tsao & McKown much in demand. With the rich nature of their backgrounds and experience, and their different talents, it has to be one of contemporary American design's most satisfying collaborations.

ABOVE LEFT The second bedroom upstairs is home to a hospital bed with a factory lamp on a homemade tripod, while an Edwardian medicine ball sits on an African stool.

ABOVE Above the bed in the master bedroom hangs a photograph by Richard Misrach. The bed cover is Provençal and by the bed sit 19th-century models of the solar system.

OPPOSITE Curling upwards from the entrance area below, the staircase has a sculpted presence. The stair treads are in Brazilian cherry wood.

Benjamin Noriega-Ortiz

"WHEN I DESIGN A HOUSE, I DESIGN IT FROM THE INSIDE OUT," SAYS BENJAMIN NORIEGA-ORTIZ. "I START BY PUTTING THE FURNITURE IN PLACE, AND THEN CREATING THE ENVELOPE FOR THE FURNITURE, AND I KEEP GOING UNTIL I GET THE HOUSE THAT I WANT. WHEN I GET THE DESIGN OF THE HOUSE, I STUDY THE SHAPE OF THE BUILDING AS A SCULPTURE, AND GO BACK IN. WE WORK FROM THE INSIDE OUT AND THE OUTSIDE IN."

And architecture and interiors have always gone hand-in-hand for Noriega-Ortiz. He was commissioned to do a house in the Bahamas for musician Lenny Kravitz – a compound of buildings within fifty acres. The plans for Kravitz (the fourth project that Noriega-Ortiz had worked on for him) included the main house, a studio, a guest house, and more. It is a miniature town, drawing on Noriega-Ortiz's training in urban design at Columbia University, as well as his degree in architecture from the University of Puerto Rico.

"I love working on a project in its entirety and building houses from the ground up," Noriega-Ortiz says. "I look at any interior project as architecture. To me planning an interior is like planning a city. As long as I can remember, since I was five or six, I wanted to be an architect. Coming from Puerto Rico, where you see very good Spanish colonial buildings it was easy to learn more about architecture than if you were living in the suburbs of America."

Noriega-Ortiz grew up within a traditional Catholic family in Puerto Rico. His father was an accountant, and looked after the books for many construction companies. In the summers Noriega-Ortiz would go with his father to sites and offices, looking over drawings and buildings, and becoming fascinated by

OPPOSITE The living room on the upper floor of the duplex flows out onto a balcony terrace. The chrome and glass table from the 1970s was found by Steven Wine in street trash waiting to be collected. The shag carpet is in wool, and the chair by Philippe Starck.

the process and mechanics of design, and spending weekends drawing and planning houses in graph books. He began studying architecture, falling in love with the work of Le Corbusier and Mies van der Rohe, fascinated particularly by the way such modernists also drew on the past, with Le Corbusier experimenting with antiques, colour, and vernacular ideas within a clean modern environment.

"Now when I look back at that, I realize that with a lot of my work I try to mix the modern and the old. I try to keep the space very modern, even if I'm using a lot of antiques. Later on, travelling in Europe, I learnt about Gaudí, and that was a great discovery, and Art Nouveau became an influence. There's actually something of every period that I like; there's no period I would say that I hate."

ABOVE A sheer curtain can be drawn across to help separate off the kitchen and dining area from the rest of the living room. The small wall-mounted bar was designed by Noriega-Ortiz and the stools are by Saarinen. The chair on the left is a custom piece from Cobweb.

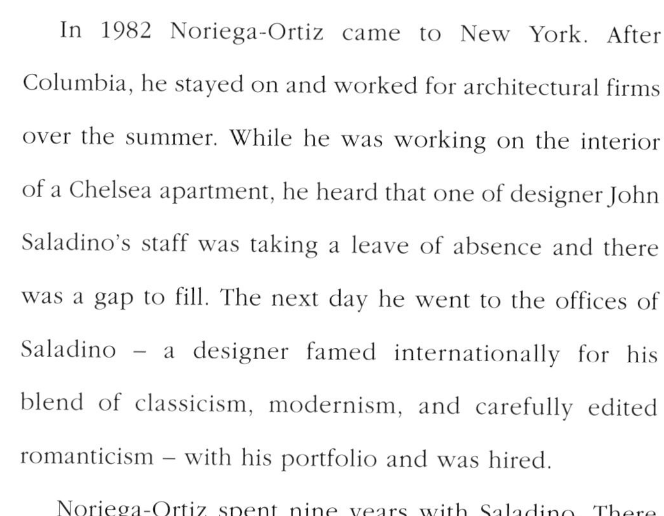

In 1982 Noriega-Ortiz came to New York. After Columbia, he stayed on and worked for architectural firms over the summer. While he was working on the interior of a Chelsea apartment, he heard that one of designer John Saladino's staff was taking a leave of absence and there was a gap to fill. The next day he went to the offices of Saladino – a designer famed internationally for his blend of classicism, modernism, and carefully edited romanticism – with his portfolio and was hired.

Noriega-Ortiz spent nine years with Saladino. There was important experience in the blending of different periods of furniture – with form and structure the common ground that bonded them together – as well as the use of colour. "Saladino was a painter who studied fine art," says Noriega-Ortiz, "and really knows how to use colour. He sees interiors as art and working with him I learnt to look at interiors as compositions; compositions that include colour, shape, and form."

Noriega-Ortiz himself, who set up his own business in 1992, has since become known for his love of monochromatic interior schemes, and his passion for texture. His favourite artist and an inspiration is Louise Nevelson, who creates monochrome sculptures in contrasting shapes and forms. Not that

Noriega-Ortiz is afraid of colour. "Monochromatic doesn't just mean that it's beige or brown," he says. "It could be red or orange. My favourite colour is blue-green – the colour of the water on the crest of the ocean. That colour to me is heaven, and that's the colour I've painted my office, and I did an apartment in New York painted entirely in that shade. To me it became a neutral. Any colour can be a neutral if you use the colour a lot."

For Mexican writer Laura Esquivel, the author of *Like Water For Chocolate*, Noriega-Ortiz created an apartment using rich Mexican colours. For his own New York apartment he wanted light, reflective tones – one hundred shades of pearl. Preferring light spaces as a reminder, and consequence of his youth in the Caribbean, the designer used sheets of mirror glass on the southern walls

BELOW The sitting room is unified by colour tone, while a range of textures provides contrast. The white lounge chair is Eero Saarinen's Womb Chair, manufactured by Knoll. The painting on the far wall is by Antoine Bootz and the sofa beneath reconditioned 1930s.

RIGHT The kitchen and dining room is differentiated from the rest of the sitting room by the terrazzo floor. The dining table, coated in vinyl, was designed by Noriega-Ortiz, while the clear chair is by Philippe Starck.

ABOVE Downstairs, the guest bedroom doubles up as a television lounge and study. The bespoke acrylic desk mounted on the windowsill was made by Plexicraft, while the chair is by Steen Ostergaard. The beds from K. Flam are also used as sofas.

of the duplex to reflect the sunlight, and then added layer upon layer of texture – constantly juxtaposing shining matt and materials – with Venetian plaster on the walls, white wool shag on the floors in the living room, and terrazzo in the kitchen, as well as splashes of chrome, glass, aluminium, and vinyl.

Texture becomes a way of differentiating one space from another. Utilitarian spaces, such as the kitchen, bathroom, and entrance hall, are marked out by terrazzo, and harder, more utilitarian materials. Elsewhere there is the highly textured carpet – a request on entering this white-on-white flat is to dispense with your footwear, putting you immediately at ease. The nature of the materials also lends glamour to the apartment, including the use of curtain fabrics, which Noriega-Ortiz also utilized to lend a light sense of separation to a space. The open-plan kitchen and dining room can be partitioned, once a meal is

LEFT In the kitchen, a mirrored splash back helps reflect light around the space; the southern walls of the apartment to the back of the stairs and foyer are also coated in mirror glass. The work tops are in Surrell, a composite material.

ABOVE The stairs are coated in a wool shag carpet and home to a chicken from American Mounted Game Birds. In the foyer guests are encouraged to remove their shoes and travel through the textured, shades of the white apartment barefoot.

over perhaps, by a diaphanous curtain. The same is true of the glass-fronted bathrooms, which can be transparent for light or curtained off for privacy.

"I love using fabrics, especially dividing rooms with translucent materials like beautiful polyesters which are easy to wash; when I use silks it's because the client wants something more upscale. What I like about using translucent fabrics for dividing rooms is that when you close them the next room goes out of focus. And texture is extremely important to me. When everything is in one colour it would be too boring if the textures aren't varied."

Noriega-Ortiz and his partner, lighting designer Steven Wine, bought the duplex in a modern, 1980s building in 2002. They were attracted by the sense of separation provided by the two floors – suggesting some of the feel of a small town-house – and a large terrace. But the apartment had been decorated

in California ranch house style, which had to go. The duplex was stripped back to its concrete roots, and the layout reordered to introduce light, and improve the foot flow around the space. The entrance foyer, bedrooms, and bathrooms are on the lower floor with the living room, kitchen, and a terrace garden above, up a flight of stairs carpeted with fluffy wool. "The most important change in the layout is that now you can always walk through to the next room – there's no room you can be trapped in with just one doorway – and so all the spaces flow together," says Noriega-Ortiz. "To me that's crucial. I don't want to be trapped in one space because I like a feeling of freedom."

Noriega-Ortiz, while developing his own furniture line, designed a number of pieces for the apartment, such as the dining table, a number of sofas, and night tables. Wine also designed lighting for the appartment, while the two also collect lights and lamps, some of which are displayed in the downstairs den – a multi-functional space, with a built-in acrylic desk by the window for home working, hidden electronics for entertainment, and day beds by Noriega-Ortiz, which can be pushed together to create a queen-sized bed for guests. Again, drapery at the doorways allows guests to separate the room off.

Given the modernity of the space, Noriega-Ortiz used fewer antiques than he might usually do. There are some early 20th-century Portuguese dining chairs, which were repainted – Noriega-Ortiz will often adapt, refinish, or refine antiques to his own use and aesthetic. Elsewhere in the mix there is a good representation of 20th-century classics: Steen Ostergard chairs from the 1970s, perspex chairs by Philippe Starck, Saarinen's Womb Chair by Knoll, as well as some of Saarinen's bar stools. The glass coffee table in the living room was found on a New York street. It's modern eclectic.

"I have more of an understanding of shapes and colours now, compared to when I started," says Noriega-Ortiz. "Being older I am more secure in my decisions and could easily show a client who is spending $2 million a table from Ikea next to an 17th-century armoire because it looks good. My interiors are like still lifes. Even if they have some fashion sense, I don't want them to be too trendy or fashionable. There should be elements from different decades. You do too many things of one period and it becomes too much of the same."

ABOVE Bedroom and bathroom are on the loyer floor of the duplex. The bed is by K. Flam, while the night tables are to Noriega-Ortiz's design. The custom-made hanging feather-shaded lights by the bed are by Steven Wine's company, And Bob's Your Uncle.

OPPOSITE The twin bathrooms sit alongside one another. They are enclosed by glass and sliding glass doors, with curtains that can be dragged across for privacy. The sink is by Kholer, the hanging lights from And Bob's Your Uncle.

Index

Selected bibliography

Molyneux, by Michael Frank (Rizzoli, 1997)
Modern, by Jonathan Glancey (Mitchell Beazley, 1999)
Rooms, by Mariette Himes Gomez (Regan Books, 2003)
I Want to Change the World, by Karim Rashid (Rizzoli, 2001)
Designing Women, by Margaret Russell (Stewart, Tabori & Chang, 2001)
Dwellings, by Stephen Sills, James Huniford & Michael Boodro (Little Brown, 2003)
The Private House, by Rose Tarlow (Clarkson Potter, 2001)
Influential Interiors, by Suzanne Trocme (Mitchell Beazley, 1999)
Juan Montoya, by Benjamin Villegas & Margaret Cottom-Winslow (Villegas Editores, 1998)
Learning To See, by Vicente Wolf (Artisan, 2002)

Addresses

BARBARA BARRY
9526 Pico Boulevard
Los Angeles, CA 90035
TEL – 310 276 9977
FAX – 310 276 9876
www.barbarabarry.com

MURIEL BRANDOLINI
525 East 72nd Street
New York, NY 10021
TEL – 212 249 4920
FAX – 212 288 6946
www.murielbrandolini.com

DAVID EASTON
Easton-Moss & Company
72 Spring Street, 7th Floor
New York, NY 10012
TEL – 212 334 3820
FAX – 212 334 3821

MICA ERTEGUN
Mac II
125 East 81st Street
New York, NY 10028
TEL – 212 249 4466

ALBERT HADLEY
24 East 64th Street
New York, NY 10021
TEL – 212 888 7979
FAX – 212 888 5597

MARIETTE HIMES GOMEZ
Gomez Associates
504-506 East 74th Street
New York, NY 10021
TEL – 212 288 6856
FAX – 212 288 1590
www.gomezassociates.com

JOANNE DE GUARDIOLA
20 East 64th Street
New York, NY 10021
TEL – 212 753 6184
FAX – 212 753 7838

KATHRYN IRELAND
1619 Stanford Street
Santa Monica, CA 90404
TEL – 310 315 4351
FAX – 310 315 4353
www.kathrynireland.com

MARTYN LAWRENCE-BULLARD
Martynus-Trip Inc
616 North Almont Drive
Los Angeles, CA 90069
TEL – 310 385 8730
FAX – 310 385 8701

LEE MINDEL
Shelton, Mindel & Associates
216 West 18th Street
New York, NY 10011
TEL – 212 243 3939
FAX – 212 727 7310

JUAN MONTOYA
330 East 59th Street, 2nd Floor
New York, NY 10022
TEL – 212 421 2400
FAX – 212 421 6240
www.juanmontoyadesign.com

JUAN PABLO MOLYNEUX
J.P. Molyneux Studio
29 East 69th Street
New York, NY 10021
TEL – 212 628 0097

BENJAMIN NORIEGA-ORTIZ
75 Spring Street, 6th Floor
New York, NY 10012
TEL – 212 343 9709
FAX – 212 343 9263
www.bnodesign.com

THOMAS PHEASANT
1029 33rd Street NW,
Washington, D.C. 20007
TEL – 202 337 6596
FAX – 202 342 3941
www.thomaspheasant.com

SILLS HUNIFORD
30 East 67th Street
New York, NY 10021
TEL – 212 988 1636
FAX – 212 988 2006

HOLLY HUNT
801 West Adams Street
Chicago, IL 60607
TEL – 312 329 5999
FAX – 312 993 0331
www.hollyhunt.com

KARIM RASHID
357 West 17th Street
New York, NY 10011
TEL – 212 929 8657
FAX – 212 929 0247
www.karimrashid.com

ROSE TARLOW
Melrose House
8454 Melrose Place
Los Angeles, CA 90069
TEL – 323 651 2202
FAX – 323 658 6548
www.rosetarlow.com

TSAO & MCKOWN
ARCHITECTS
20 Vandam Street, 10th Floor
New York, NY 10013
TEL – 212 337 2617
FAX – 212 337 0013
www.tsao-mckown.com

Acknowledgements

Dominic Bradbury and Mark Luscombe-Whyte would like to thank all of the designers who have appeared in this book, and their staff, for their support and hospitality.

Thanks also to all at Pavilion and Vendome, particularly Mark Magowan and family, and to Helen Auerbach, Faith Bradbury, Karen Howes, Jonny Pegg and Curtis Brown, Matthew Smyth, Marie Valensi, Eugenie Voorhees.